WALK WITH GOD

WALK WITH GOD

*Wisdom and Guidance
to Help Us in Our Daily Lives*

FULTON J. SHEEN

ST PAULS

Library of Congress Cataloging-in-Publication Data

Sheen, Fulton J. (Fulton John), 1895-1979.
  Walk with God: wisdom and guidance to help us in our daily lives / Fulton J. Sheen.
    p. cm.
  Originally published: New York: Maco Magazine Corp., 1965.
  ISBN 978-0-8189-1267-2
  1. Christian life—Catholic authors.   I. Title.
  BX2350.3.S53 2008
  248.4'82—dc22
                                         2008003232
Nihil Obstat:
John A. Goodwine, JCD
Censor Librorum
Imprimatur:
✠ Terence J. Cooke, VG
New York, September 19, 1965

The Nihil Obstat and Imprimatur are official declarations that a book
or pamphlet is free of doctrinal or moral error. No implication is contained
therein that those who have granted the Nihil Obstat and Imprimatur
agree with the contents, opinions or statements expressed.

Walk with God was originally published in 1965 by Maco Magazine Corporation,
757 Third Ave., New York, N.Y. 10017. This edition is published by special arrange-
ment with the Society for the Propagation of the Faith,
366 Fifth Avenue, New York, NY 10001 in collaboration with the Fulton J. Sheen
Foundation of Perth, Australia. Printed in the U.S.A.

Produced and designed in the United States of America by the
Fathers and Brothers of the Society of St. Paul,
2187 Victory Boulevard, Staten Island, New York 10314-6603
as part of their communications apostolate.

ISBN-10: 0-8189-1267-7
ISBN-13: 978-0-8189-1267-2

Printing Information:

Current Printing - first digit	2	3	4	5	6	7	8	9	10

Year of Current Printing - first year shown

	2014	2015	2016	2017

Table of Contents

Turning from the Road of Evil Intent

Turning from the Road of Conceit

The Way of Blessedness

The Four Roads

There are four types of persons who miss their mark in the world, as revealed in the parables of the lost sheep, the lost coins, and the prodigal son and the elder son.

Some are lost through stupidity and thoughtlessness, like sheep who do not intentionally go astray.

The second type of errant soul is illustrated in the parable of the lost coins. Sheep may lose themselves, but a coin is not lost through its own fault, but generally through carelessness of others. To this group belong many delinquent children whom parental carelessness allowed to roll into the streets and to become lost.

A third class, described in the parable of the prodigal son, is composed of those who go astray neither through heedlessness nor through the fault of others, but with deliberate choice. Refusing to accept parental discipline, they ask for a share of money to enjoy what is called their "own freedom" and to make their "own life" as the prodigal did who went off into a foreign country.

The fourth class is illustrated in the same parable by the elder son who is unconscious that he is a sinner, though all too conscious of the sin of his brother. There was no record in the story as told by Our Lord that the younger son had wasted his substance on harlots, but when the elder son protested he inserted that charge. Neither does he speak of his brother, but he speaks of the "father's son," thereby indicating that he had lost all social sense. The parable of the prodigal son is, therefore, the story of two sons who lost their father's love: one because he was too good and the other because he was too bad.

But there is hope for each one of them. In the first instance, the shepherd, when he finds the lost sheep, puts it upon his shoulders and rejoices, though there was no record that he rejoiced in the possession of the ninety-nine that were not lost. What is it that makes the Divine Shepherd so agitated and sad in heart at the loss of just one, when he has so many? Very likely because it was his property, and also because of his great compassion for men who have lost their way. Putting it upon his shoulders was a rest-giving act, very likely needful to the poor sheep which could go no further and was faint and weary.

The parable of the lost coins in part implies that every coin bore upon itself some image, as the Roman coin had Caesar's image upon it and the coin which Jacob paid for a debt was stamped with a lamb. The implication here is that every man is made to the image and likeness of God, and once again what is introduced is the note of proprietorship. The woman who found the coin lighted the candle and swept the house, which would represent the disturbance of settled opinion and practices, and the turning of the soul upside down to indicate a willingness to have a present order disturbed in order to save one lost man. When the coin is found all the neighbors are called in to rejoice, though there is no indication that there was such a celebration in the possession of the other nine. Joy is necessarily social, or as someone has put it: "Happiness is born a twin!" and we must share it with others.

The prodigal son returned to the father's house because of emptiness in his soul. Recognition of his guilt preceded a true restoration. Up to this point he had lived "outside" of himself; now in the language of the Gospel he "enters into himself," that is, begins to reflect and to see his true nature.

When he starts back, he finds that the father is not in his own house, but is out on the roadway ready to welcome him back. Forgiveness meets us more than halfway. The kiss of welcome is extended before one word of penitence or request had been spoken. Then comes the feast where Heaven keeps holiday, when some poor waif comes slinking back to the Father.

The elder son represents those who are rather resentful of the mercy extended to others. Even though the elder son had remained home, it was a thankless service; there was no glow of family love to warm it and never once did he realize the beauties of sonship. Many are cradled in the sacred associations of the Church, but it is not a loving service, but only a duty. There are souls within the Kingdom of God who are not fully in sympathy with the greatness of Divine Love.

BOOKS BY BISHOP SHEEN

The Armor of God

Calvary and the Mass

Children and Parents

Communism and the Conscience
of the West

The Cross and the Beatitudes

The Cross and the Crisis

A Declaration of Dependence

The Divine Romance

The Divine Verdict

The Eternal Galilean

For God and Country

Freedom under God

God and Intelligence

God and War

Guide to Contentment

Liberty, Equality and Fraternity

The Life of All Living

Lift Up Your Heart

Love One Another

Moods and Truths

The Moral Universe

The Mystical Body of Christ

Old Errors and New Labels

Peace of Soul

Philosophies at War

The Philosophy of Religion

The Philosophy of Science

The Prodigal World

The Rainbow of Sorrow

Religion Without God

The Rock Plunged Into Eternity

The Seven Capital Sins

The Seven Last Words

Seven Pillars of Peace

The Seven Virtues

Seven Words to the Cross

Those Mysterious Priests

Thoughts for Daily Living

Victory Over Vice

Walk with God

The Way of the Cross

Way to Happiness

Way to Inner Peace

Whence Come Wars

You

WALK WITH GOD

Turning from the Road of Confusion

The shepherd, when he finds the lost sheep,
puts it upon his shoulders and rejoices.

Drift

One of the finest chapters in the ten-volume *Study of History* by Arnold Toynbee is the one on the "Sense of Drift." He defines it as a carelessness about the loss of spiritual and moral growth. It is, to his mind, one of the most painful of tribulations that afflict the souls of men and women in an age of social decay. His explanation for it is that it is a punishment for the sin of idolatry, or the worship of the creature instead of the Creator.

The most classic example of drifting is that of the rudderless ship, which, to Plato, represented the chaos of the universe abandoned by God. In individual lives, drifting is the failure to offer any kind of resistance to a current. Icebergs drift; that is why they are destroyed. They eventually get out of the cold waters which sustain them into the warm waters which melt them.

There are certain characteristics of drifting:

I. It is hardly at first noticed by the person himself. Others see it in us more quickly than we see it ourselves. Youths are often surprised when elders with vaster experience point out with exactness their destiny and future. Studies on juvenile delinquency suggest that a life of crime can be predicted at the age of twelve.

2. Drifting is always from a higher to a lower stage, from the Divine to the human level, from the order of faith to the order of reason, from reason to senses and from senses to animalism. No one ever drifted into virtue, but anyone can drift into vice. This is because there is within every human heart a tendency toward decay, which begins to operate if it is not resisted. A man who is poisoned may be brought an antidote. It makes little difference whether he throws the antidote out of the window or whether he pours it on the floor or whether he ignores it. The poison which he has in his body operates by the mere fact that he has neglected to take the remedy.

3. The most tragic cases of drifting are those who have had the most talents and perhaps even a high standard of virtue. *Corruptio optimi pessima*: "The corruption of the best is the worst." The fair and pure lily smells the foulest when it loses its freshness. As Shakespeare put it: "Loathsome canker lives in sweetest bud."

What is curious about all who drift is that eventually they begin to say that they are under the control of fate, necessity or cruel destiny, in order to relieve themselves of responsibility. A scapegoat must be found to ease the conscience. If the drifter ever blames himself, it is in order that he may be praised. The man who drifts prides himself that he is at liberty at all times. But he forgets that, building his morality on subjective judgments of value, he leaves himself utterly defenseless against the onslaughts of cruder men who proclaim their own subjective standards by violence. The violent man says he is better because stronger:

> Pale Ebenezer thought it wrong to fight
> But roaring Bill, who killed him, thought it right.

The principal cause of drift in individuals is the absence of a goal or a purpose in life. He who has no target is not so apt to shoot arrows. Matches are not carried long that have nothing to ignite. The uncommitted mind is the drifting mind — it floats down stream with public opinion. "They say," or "They are wearing green this year," or "Oh gosh, mom all the kids are wearing them." The terrible anonymous authority of "they" carries along the dead minds that are too lazy to think for themselves.

The committed mind, with a purpose and a faith, limits all those possibilities which distract from attaining his goal; he knows that the grain of seed must fall into the ground and die in a certain fashion before new life can spring forth.

Nothing that drifts can reverse itself except by a force outside itself. A ball thrown across the room will not be reversed in direction except by a power greater than itself. In like manner, a Divine Power called "grace" is necessary to stop decay. Nor does this come unless asked for: "Ask and you shall receive." Paul, who was drifting into a violent persecutor, became a zealous apostle; Peter, who was drifting into apostasy, became the Rock and the Shepherd. No one need remain what he is. A saint asked God why He did not pardon the devil. God answered: "Because he never asked Me."

Closed Doors

We judge men by the evil they have done, but rarely by the good they have left undone. The evil in man's life can often be undone; for example, his dishonesty can be atoned for by kindness to the poor. But the good which has been left undone is often like a spent arrow. School days, youth, opportunities for study, parental training — these things have seasons and, like springtime, quickly pass. There is such a thing as "closed doors."

In the parable of the ten virgins, there is implied considerable morality on the part of them all. But five were wise and five were foolish. The hour of the marriage approached, but the five had not availed themselves of every opportunity to provide enough oil. Then came a moment when the "doors were shut." It was customary in the East, at great entertainments, to close the doors when all the guests had assembled. As St. Augustine put it: "No enemy got in, no friend got out." Lamps that should have been provided with oil were empty. Opportunity had passed.

The extinction of the oil came about by doing nothing. No positive sin is alleged against the foolish virgins. They had not ridiculed the necessity of working hard; they were just heedless, and for that reason have been labeled "foolish." White fences become black fences in time; clocks not wound refuse to say: "Time is passing"; neglect to put oil in the motor is like the virgins not putting oil in the lamps — one never gets to his destination. Water in a pond that is never stirred produces a green scum and a foul odor. No positive wickedness is necessary to spoil human character; neglect alone will do it.

It has been said that inside of every fat man is a thin man trying to get out. He never gets out because of omitting to diet. Fat, ignorance, stiffened muscles, craving for alcohol, creep on from day to day by the mere fact that we allowed our lamp to smoke, flicker and finally die. No great crime was laid at the feet of the travelers who passed by the wounded man on the road to Jericho — but only that they passed by. There is no point in asking what they did wrong. They did nothing wrong; but neither did they do anything right. They "passed by on the other side." No oppressive wrongs are mentioned against the rich man in the Gospel. He just neglected the opportunity to help the beggar at the door. On the Last Day too, the indictment of the evil will be neglect, because they saw the hungry and gave not to eat; the thirsty and gave not to drink.

No positive dishonor is laid at the door of the man who buried his talent in a napkin, except that he did nothing with it. He was a good-for-nothing servant. The salt which lost its savor is to be cast out. The young man who told the Lord that he had kept all the commandments from youth was still lacking something — namely a glow, a fervor and an interest in others. He was to do something positive, for example, to sell some of his goods, for he was rich, and help the poor. In every instance, the condemnation is because "they did nothing"

— empty lamps, buried napkins, sterile virtue, unused salt and services neglected.

It could very well be that in our moral instruction we are emphasizing too much not doing wrong and forgetting the necessity of doing good. "Thou shalt not" belongs to law. "Thou shalt" belongs to grace. That was why Our Lord added a new commandment to the ten which He called "new," and it began with "Thou shalt" — love God, love neighbor. Accent the positive. In the Sermon on the Mount, the workers of iniquity are those who hear His words and do them not. The pitying Judge of all humanity is tender to those who are led astray by ignorance or who fall by sins; but severe to those who do nothing. The greatest inhumanity that can be ascribed to men is having an opportunity for doing good to others and doing nothing. The serious sin is not always one of commission, but omission. In fact, this is the way Scripture describes the loss of our eternal soul: "How shall we escape, if we neglect so great a salvation?"

The Peril of the Second Best

Very few ever choose that which is intrinsically evil. Rather, most people are subject to the temptation of choosing the better instead of the best, fitting in with the average rather than with the creative minority.

In the parable of the talents in the Gospel, one was given five talents, another two and another one; all were asked to trade with them. These need not be understood only in terms of talents of money, but even as capacities, or gifts of nature. The man who received five talents made another five; the man who received the two made another two, each one returning 100 per cent on gifts God gave him. He who received the one talent, however, did nothing with it.

The two-talent man is the average man, not very conscious of superiority over the great mass of his fellow creatures, not claiming a right to the five talents nor linking himself with those who have only one. But he who received the one, feeling that it was below even the average man, did not attempt to make any return on his gift. He may have justified himself on the ground that it was so little it was not worth bothering with: "Well, I am doing nothing wrong." But he forgot that gifts are forfeited by disuse, as the Lord said to him: "Take the talent away."

In the parable, he tried to excuse his indolence on the

ground that the master was hard and too exacting. It could sometimes be that those who receive small gifts are apt to be depressed by their insignificance and to consider them valueless, and give up the effort of enriching and increasing them. The real point of the parable seems to be that he actually played the part of the idler just because he was the man who might be thought to be the most excusable.

But negligence is inexcusable, and he is condemned for being unprofitable, for he advanced neither his master's interests not his own, which were bound up with one another. It is a very fearful thought that not for any crime or offense against the common laws of God and man is he condemned, but just simply for idleness and omission of duty.

Spiritual indolence and the refusal of a man to better himself spiritually can be reckoned as serious a fault as active wickedness, and meet with similar judgment.

The ground of Divine rewards are in the service rendered and not in the work itself. Thus, they who produce great results will not be honored more than those people who produce less striking results. The poor, simple, uneducated people with one talent who are equally faithful with smaller gifts will receive the same reward. It is not the ownership of talents that determines the judgment, but rather the enrichment of any talent that one possesses. Because one cannot do much, one is not excused from doing little. Condemnation awaits the man who refuses to help because he could not lead. The miserable fear of being mediocre cripples good work and the great reward. What is not increased, decreases. The man who improves his gifts, however small, will surely obtain the Kingdom of God. Only what we use becomes crystallized into character. To do no harm is praise fit for a stone, but not for a man.

Gradual Decline

Do men suddenly become wicked or evil? Edmund Burke, in one of his classical speeches of English political literature, discusses this in relation to the decline of virtue in a politician: "I believe," he wrote, "the instances are exceedingly rare of men immediately passing over a clear and marked line of virtue into declared vice and corruption. There are a sort of middle tints and shades between the two extremes; there is something uncertain on the confines of the two empires which they must first pass through, and which renders the change easy and imperceptible. There are even a sort of impositions so well contrived that, at the very time the path of rectitude is quitted forever, men seem to be advancing into some higher and nobler road of public conduct."

Not only in political but in social activity as well, there is a kind of a "no man's land" between goodness and wickedness; one does not go to bed one night a saint and wake up the next morning as a devil. Between the realms of black and white there is the grey confusion of a barely perceptible decline. Samson, after many moral lapses, was unconscious that his strength was lost.

Moral decline often brings with it mental indecision. This is illustrated in the history of the Israelites at the time they were led by the great prophetess, Deborah. Barak, the great soldier that he was, refused to lead the 10,000 men against the enemy unless Deborah went with him to victory. But there was one town, Meroz, which hung back and refused to fight. Hidden away in a safe valley, it ignored patriotic duty even in time of danger. The Angel of the Lord pronounced a curse upon that village which had neglected its duty: "Curse ye the land of Meroz. Cursed the inhabitants thereof because they have not come to the help of the Lord, to help His most valiant men." The land of Meroz was not a traitor nor a spy, nor did it aid the foe. It did not quickly pass from light to darkness, but rather it slowly took a position in which it was neither on this side nor that. It did nothing. And for that reason will it always appear as a shirker. Vice sometimes conquers because the virtuous are inactive.

In the life of every character there is an hour of crucial test, when the line is crossed without any great fanfare or open decision, but where the hidden state of the soul remains manifest. As Margaret Sackville put it:

> *And ever more we sought the fight, but still*
> *Some pale enchantment clouded all our will*
> *So that we faltered; even when the foe*
> *Lay, at our sudden onset crushed and low,*
> *As a flame dies, so passed our wrath away —*
> *And fatal to us was the battle day.*

Many lose their peace of soul on earth and their soul for eternity, not just because of the evil they have done, but also because of the good that they have left undone. A man who is poisoned may have the antidote alongside his bed, but if he neglects to take it, he perishes.

The muscles unused stiffen; the talents unused are taken away; flight from battle turns into defeat. The self-indulgent indolence makes one indifferent to duty and eventually prepares for that slow descent into the region of the darkened spirit. Nations and persons do not become reprobates and delinquents all at once. The process of decay is usually gradual and proceeds from one lost opportunity to another, until the fate is sealed and the doom goes forth. "Curse ye Meroz." Could this be the reason that the Last Judgment is pictured in Scripture as sudden, and without warning — because there had been so many little twinges of conscience ignored, that a great warning would not change them any more than it did the multitudes at the time of the Flood? There may be a profound spiritual therapeutic in the nightly examination of conscience; it enables us to take two steps backward for the one we stepped forward to the abyss.

Beatniks and Hermits

There is a definite resemblance between beatniks and hermits. Although the two are poles apart and the similarity is superficial, it is there. Both are in flight from a world. Both left civilization: one for the desert; the other for a cellar. Both are products of their respective ages.

In the past, a man who fled the society of his fellows to dwell in solitude was a hermit. A man who in the same way flees society today is called a beatnik. They look alike. Bearded, unkempt, dirty, thin, and dressed in rags, they scorn even the basic social conventions of the society each has rejected. They act alike; live solitary lives, shedding attachment for all material things, scrounging for food. But they are alike only up to a point. There is actually a vast world of difference between the two, and the difference lies in the "why" each did what he did.

The hermit rebelled from a world of persecution or corruption that would not allow him to live for God. His was a positive vocation. Affirming his belief in the importance of being God-centered, he retreated in protest from a world that was not.

The beatnik, on the other hand, has not a vocation, but

an avocation; a calling-away from his ordinary activity. He retreats from the world which surrounds him, confused by its meaningless extremes of affluence and poverty. Rebelling against a life with no purpose, he creates his own purpose, and his life comes to revolve only around himself — all things having meaning only as they are related to him.

There is another element essential to the motivation of both beatnik and hermit. It is the degree of consciousness of their belief which separates the beatnik and the hermit from the average man. Only a man deeply conscious of his mission as a Christian on earth would leave a world of comfort and convenience for a cave. In the same way, only an individual deeply troubled by life's apparent fruitlessness and relativity would leave the shelter of human respect and common courtesies to move restlessly along the road of life. Although both have taken extreme roads, both have a human heart for love. The hermit, however, realized with Saint Augustine that God has made us for Himself, and our "hearts are restless 'til they rest in Him." By renouncing all things human, he found peace.

The beatnik looking for love thinks of it primarily as physical, whose peak is reached when a great intensity of reciprocal emotion is felt. Being sensory, it is transitory, and so the beatnik flies from partner to partner, adding zero to zero, hoping to find something in the end which can be added. Restlessness and a continuous search is his constant frustration. What he has is not love, but sex. For love concentrates on the object, sex concentrates on the subject. Love is directed to someone else for the sake of the other's perfection; sex is directed to self for the sake of self-satisfaction. The ego in sex pleads that it loves the alter ego, but what it loves is really the possibility of its own pleasure in the other ego. The other person is necessary for the return of the egotist upon himself. Refusing to be related to anything else, he soon sees that nothing is for him.

So the beatnik ends by hating self in an agony of unanswered questions, while the hermit ends by loving God in perfect peace. More telling than anything else perhaps, is what each produces: the hermit, more often than not, a saint; the beatnik, a jungle of abstract art and a mumble of meaningless poetry.

Neither is suited to our times because it is the world that has to be saved — not by flight from its paganism nor its affluence, but by supra-worldliness in the world.

Sadness and Doubt

It would be an interesting psychological study to discover the relationship between a man's doubts and his melancholy, between his want of conviction about the meaning of life and his sadness of heart. There is no doubt that when a man loses his faith and his morals, he falls into the pit of cynicism, and when a man begins to possess his soul, he feels an exhilaration of heart.

Everyone knows Thomas the Doubter. He was certainly a skeptic, but he was also lugubrious and sad. As a boy Thomas must always have expected that it would rain the day of the picnic; he must have loved dark days, rainy nights and black moods. He must have been a man very close to the earth, not in the sense of being practical, but because the material, the physical, the tangible, the earthly alone could give him some assurance of spiritual truths. This being so, it is very likely that his moodiness and sadness and melancholy were the cause of his doubts.

Take the occasion when Our Lord was beyond the Jordan. Messengers announced to Him: "He whom You love is sick" — the particular friend being Lazarus whom the Lord was later to raise from the dead. Two days later, the news came that Lazarus was dead. Here we heard the gloomy Thomas speak: "Let us go too and be killed along with Him." Thomas knew that if Our Lord went to Jerusalem that He would be killed. And that would be the end of Him. Death is all there is. Though there was devotion to Christ, it went no further than His life. All His teachings about Resurrection and His Kingdom enduring to the end of time were swallowed up in gloom. He saw all the crude, material forces, a stone as a stone, a death as a death. If the Divine Master was to have a dead end, namely, being killed, well then, let us all be killed.

The same sadness came out at the Last Supper on the night before Our Lord's death when He said that He was going to prepare a home for His Apostles and all who believed in Him. Then recalling His three years teaching, He said to them: "You know where it is I am going, and you know the way there." The despondency of Thomas burst out as he looked into the face of Our Lord and said that he did not know the way. The harp of his life had only minor chords, and he plucked them once again.

Melancholy is probably the reason why he was absent at the first appearance of the risen Lord. Always expecting the worst, he was sure that his Lord had failed and that the Crucifixion had voided all His promises. Finally, the despairing state of mind produced ultimate skepticism as he refused to believe the testimony of the other Apostles and witnesses, saying: "Until I have seen the mark of the nails in His Hands, until I have put my finger into the mark of the nails, and put my hand into His Side, you will never make me believe."

Dante was right. One may sink into the invincible habit of doubt and unbelief by simply encouraging within oneself a sad or dismal view of things. But the sweet medicine of the Divine

Presence a week later cured his sadness of soul, as the Divine Master told him to put his finger into His Hand, and his hand into His Side to be cured of his doubts. When Thomas was all darkness, the Lord put into his hand a telescope through which he peered to see the stars of Scars won in the battle with evil. All his doubts vanished and he threw himself on his knees before the Resurrection and the Life crying: "My Lord and My God." He was the first after the Resurrection to pronounce the word "God" and to confess the full Divinity of Christ. On the rebound from doubt, he achieved the pinnacle of faith.

Little consolation is afforded in the character of this man for those who feel that a constant attitude of doubting, a refusal to come to grips with the meaning of existence, is a mark of intellectuality and the tone of a speculative mind. No, rather the doubter reaches that condition through pessimism and sadness. Skepticism is, as a matter of fact, not an intellectual position at all; it is a moral position. It comes from the way one lives, or it comes from the failure to act on that which we already believe. It would be very satisfying to have some description of Thomas after the Resurrection. One wonders if he did not become one of the happiest and most joyful of all the Apostles. He must have been, for he died a martyr, and only joyful souls ever go to their death for the sake of Love Divine.

Making Up One's Mind

Is there any relationship between the inability of many to make up their minds and the increase in mental breakdowns in our civilization? More and more people are finding it difficult to make decisions. Many are like the tramp who was hired by a farmer to put potatoes in three piles. On the pile on the right, he was to put the good potatoes; on the pile on the left, the rotten potatoes; on a pile in the center, he was to place those in which the good part of the potato could be cut out from the bad. After an hour, the tramp came to the farmer saying: "I give up on this job. This making decisions is driving me crazy."

Indecisiveness comes in part from a denial of truth. The mind necessarily remains uncommitted when it sees no ideal worth following. When one has no target, why shoot the arrow? One idea is just as good as another then. There is no reason for deciding on one rather than the other. Some minds are like museums — full of a haphazard collection of views and impressions which they pick up like they do a singing commercial, but which they never act upon. Wordsworth well described the man of decision:

Who, with a natural instinct to discern
What knowledge can perform, is diligent to learn;

Abides by this resolve, and stops not there,
But makes his moral being his prime care.
Who, if he be called upon to face
Some awful moment to which Heaven has joined
Great issues, good or bad for humankind,
Is happy as a lover: and attired
With sudden brightness, like a man inspired;
And through the height of conflict keeps the law
In calmness made, and sees what he foresaw;
Or if an unexpected call succeed,
Come when it will, is equal to the need.

Another reason for the inability to come to grips with life is a want of morality and decency. He who enjoys the ill-gotten gains of dishonesty finds it very difficult to decide in favor of honesty. Every decision in the moral order demands some kind of renunciation. The pursuit of political power, for example, is not compatible with indolence. The refusal to give up the lesser thing to find the better produces this double-mindedness or "two-souled" character, who is always wavering and irresolute with no definite principle and stable vocation. On the inside, such a character is very much like an orchestra and two conductors, both directing at the same time but from totally different scores of music.

On the more positive side, the decisive man cannot bear to sit amidst unrealized speculations. To him, speculation is valid only for doing. This does not mean that the decisive man is all action and no thinking, for sudden resolutions, like a sudden rise and fall of the mercury in a barometer, indicate little else than the changeableness of mental weather. Some men are very decisive without being wise, holding often to a plan when wisdom would have recommended its being abandoned. Thomas Aquinas gave the proper relation between thinking and action: "Begin doing the good to others upon which you have already meditated."

In the realm of the religious and moral, one of the most interesting examples of a man who failed to carry through what his mind saw was Agrippa, who said to Paul: "You have almost persuaded me to become a Christian." Life is a visitation; some opportunities are of a richer, rarer kind, in which we receive calls more solemn, weighty and decisive. Such was the summons to Agrippa, but he proved to be one of that great army of the "almost persuaded," among whom were Lot's wife; Pharaoh; the rich young ruler who would not give up his property; the foolish virgins; Herod who beheaded John; Judas and Pilate who confessed the innocence of Our Lord and betrayed and condemned Him; Felix who trembled; and now Agrippa, who was called upon not so much to decide the prisoner's fate as his own.

Nothing makes for the committed mind as faith, and nothing leaves a man so singularly defenseless against the violence of others as those who accept no authority and no moral standards. If one point of view is just as good as another, then the crude man of strength, the dictator, will make up their minds. Pragmatism, or the denial of truth, is the vestibule to Communism.

Singleness of Purpose

It has been said that if you want anything done, go to a busy man. This is true. The lazy man never has any spare time, because any work he is asked to do is an interruption to his indolence. The busy man, being used to doing things, is never taken by surprise by a request. His secret of getting anything done is to know what to leave undone. The busier one becomes, the more he has to build a pyramid of priorities, deciding that the unimportant will give way to the important.

The son of Confucius once said to him: "I apply myself with diligence to every kind of study, neglect nothing that could render me clever and brilliant; but I do not advance." "Omit some of your pursuits," replied Confucius, "and you will get on better. Among those who travel on foot, have you ever seen any who run? It is essential to do everything in order, and to grasp that which is within the reach of your arm; otherwise, you give yourself useless trouble. Those who, like yourself, desire to do everything in one day, do nothing to the end of their lives, while others who steadily adhere to one pursuit find that they have accomplished their purpose." Douglas Woodruff, speaking of those who love confused hurry, said: "The reason Americans do not like Rome is they heard it was not built in a day."

Progress is much more than motion. Youth is fond of speed in order that the acceleration of the means may make atonement for the want of an end or a purpose. Chesterton once said that the only thing that never makes any progress is the idea of progress. Unless we have a fixed goal, we would never know we were advancing toward the goal. Rivers make progress toward the sea, but as they do they grow not shallower, but deeper.

In the moral order, continuous progress is difficult. The Israelites were once within eleven miles of the Promised Land. Because of a moral failure, it took forty years to enter Canaan. In the spiritual order, there is often a slipping back, a falling away, a retreat after an advance and a collapse after a momentary enthusiasm.

Character is to some extent judged by what a man does with his falls. A pig falls into the mud and stays there; a sheep falls in and climbs out. Dissatisfaction with one's spiritual state is the first step toward improvement. To stay complacently where one is in the religious life, is as if a tree should congratulate itself on being no higher than a shrub.

One often wonders what a saint is like. A saint is one who puts forth the same amount of energy in developing justice, charity, joy and peace as the very prosperous business man puts forth in making money. It may even take less energy to be a saint than to be a millionaire, because the saint is assured of the help of God, while the millionaire is not because he has to rely on his own efforts. Leon Bloy once wrote that the greatest tragedy in all the world is not being a saint. He did not put the sanctity very far beyond the reach of anyone when he added: "One step beyond mediocrity, and we are saints."

Even the most ordinary life is filled with impressive experiences. Every temptation to an evil temper is an opportunity to decide whether we shall gain the calmness and rest of Christ, or whether we shall be tossed by the restlessness and agitation of the world. Infinite as are the varieties of life, so manifold are the paths to saintly character; and he who has not found out directly or indirectly to make everything converge toward his soul's sanctification has as yet missed the meaning of life — and its happiness too.

This does not mean the saint does not busy himself with the world. He does, *but not* in the same way as a worldly man. The saint treats the world like a ship. The world must not be in him as the water must not be in the ship; but he makes spiritual progress in the world as the ship advances thanks to the water. Two extremes are possible in deciding what is relevant to our life. One is: "I am too busy to pray." The other is to say: "It is time to pray. I cannot help you out of the ditch." The one who never prays will soon give up helping the fallen out of ditches, as he who neglects loving his neighbor will eventually cease loving God. The one supreme business of life is saving our soul. If that is lost, everything is lost. But by a curious paradox, they serve the world who are most impressed with the words of our Lord: "What does it profit a man if he gain the whole world and suffers the loss of his soul?"

The busy man, being used to doing things
is never taken by surprise by a request.

Manners

There was a barn near where I lived as a boy, in which a troublesome horse was kept. The horse had the habit of kicking anyone who came in back of his stall. The owner would always say in excuse: "He doesn't mean anything."

Discourteous manners may not have behind them intentional injury, but they still give pain, like the kick of the horse. Let others debate whether politeness and courtesy are passing out of the world; better it would be to affirm the beauty of courtesy as one of the nobler forms of unselfishness. It does not restrict itself to a class or to those whom we seek to influence, nor is it taken off with dress clothes. It is not always the intellectuals who are most courteous, sometimes moral meanness can exist side by side with education. True courtesy presupposes good will toward all others, particularly in trifles. In matters that are indifferent, it accommodates itself to others.

Everyone carries with him or her a certain moral atmosphere which others breathe in as they come in contact. The gentle considerateness of some adds to the moral tone of society, while the want of politeness drags it down.

One of the very courteous men in Scripture was Boaz, who asked that the reapers in the field should leave some sheaves for Ruth that she might pick them up, as if they had not been left there on purpose.

One also finds another perfect example of courtesy in Paul's Letter to Philemon, which is his only personal and private letter that has been preserved. Paul begs the slave owner to show favor and affection for a poor, runaway, thievish servant. Saint Francis of Assisi said: "Courtesy is one of the properties of God Who gives His sun and rain to the just and the unjust by courtesy; and courtesy is the sister of charity, by which hatred is extinguished and love is cherished."

Courtesy which is shown on the surface, without love, is like giving alms for the sake of being seen. It may make a little difference to the giver, but it makes much difference to the receiver. Politeness that degenerates into flattery or a hypocritical gentleness adds no content to the sum total of the world's love.

General Lee was one day in a railway car going to Richmond and was seated at the end farthest from the door. The other seats were filled with officers and soldiers. An old woman, poorly dressed entered at one of the stations and, finding no seat and none having been offered her, she went to the rear of the car. Lee immediately stood up and gave her his seat. Instantly, one officer after another arose to offer the seat to Lee who said: "No gentlemen, if there was no seat for this infirm old lady, there can be none for me."

Familiarity is always in danger of swallowing up courtesy. A husband and wife who become used to each other are apt to slip into a rudeness, and later on, to a brutality which is born of not appreciating the blessings that are daily. Some men who are bears at home appear as gentle as lambs when they meet their superior in the business world. But such gentleness is not benevolence, for no greatness can awe politeness into servility, and no intimacy can sink it into coarse familiarity. Religion should make us the most polite creatures in the world, and he who is not polite may well have his religion suspected, for if the heart is in love with God, how can it not show that love to every man?

Holiness

Why does Christianity have so little appeal today? It is the one religion in the world which claims to give not just a new emotional outlook on the world, but the power to become a new and different creature. If the claim is so great, and the fact is so overwhelming in those who have experienced it, why so much indifference?

One reason is it is easy to be a materialist or idealist, a Communist or anti-Communist, for these leave our personal morals to our subjective judgments. If I say a yard is twenty-one inches, then to deny it is to be accused of intolerance. But Christianity makes terrific demands on our lower nature, and the price to pay for peace of soul is too great. But there is another reason not to be sought in the escapism of the cowardly but rather within religion itself. One perhaps would be in the right direction if he started with the proposition that today practically all men have heard the arguments for Christianity, even though they got them in a distorted way. Furthermore, reason today rarely convinces anyone; it was Hitler who said that people are so dumb that they are guided by emotion, which in turn is fed by repetition. That is why in advertising one hears commercials endlessly repeated over and over. No argument

— just the tick of the emotional clock, the slow dripping of water on the head until the purchaser is conditioned.

If, then, minds today are not led by that noble faculty which makes tracks to the moon, one has yet to find the one argument that is not an argument at all in the strict sense of the word, but bowls them over by the impact of its unanswerability and truth — and that is the argument of holiness. Sanctity alone can convince minds that are looking for truth, hearts that are looking for love and emotions that have been broken by fear.

Violence convinces no one of the untruth of Communism, because it is unholy. But holiness does, because it is not on the surface like pietistic gestures, but in the depths inspiring every action and thought. Botanists tell us that the lower order of plants produce their seed on the surface of their leaves. But the higher one ascends in the kingdom of vegetation, the deeper is the seed embedded in its covering. Superficial religion or professional religion may argue and even be worn on the sleeve, but holy religion is so deep that it causes reverence, awe and desire in those who see it.

The world today needs saints. We have plenty of knowledge, power and education. But our education is not bringing us to the knowledge of the truth, and power is preparing to destroy all power. It is not enough to have one or two men in the world who are saints, but dozens. These men would not hide themselves in the desert or cloister or sanctuary, except for the early hours of the morning and the late hours of the night; but all the rest of the day they would be spending themselves and being spent on neighbor. Their preaching would be in their example, and their arguments would be their own inner joy. Their reputation would be such that the others would say of them as the girl said of Peter: "You have been with the Galilean."

Sanctity means separation from the spirit of the world, with immersion in the activity of the world. Saints would be in the world, not of it; they would have no public relation boosters to publicize them; they would never ask for money; perhaps the one venture which would stand out most in their lives would be poverty of spirit. Since they would have nothing, others would look to their being for their real worth and wish they had their joy and contentment. "The Communist hates God; the poet seeks God; the preacher proclaims God; the saint exhibits God."

Holiness is the only means by which morality can be diffused. It is like salt; its usefulness to others must begin with self. As the wise man imparts wisdom, so the saint imparts saintliness.

Gandhi's power was not in his non-violence, but in his poverty of spirit and holiness. Pope John XXIII's power was not in his pontifical office, but in his saintly humanism, which stretched out his arms like the fleshy columns of Bernini to embrace all mankind in his grasp. Maybe the reason this chapter was written on holiness was to convince myself how much I need it. Pray for me.

Turning
from the Road
of Misguidance

The parable of the lost coin implies…
A willingness to have a present order disturbed
in order to save one lost man.

Love's Promises

Every man and woman in love promise each other something that only God can give. It is as if each were giving the other a title to a river which emptied into the ocean.

Why is love so rich in promise and so miserly in fulfillment? The promise is in the future and therefore is infinite in possibilities; the present is "cabined, cribbed, confined," and hence finite in realization. Because every lover thinks that love is like an electric switch which each turns on to produce the light and heat of love, never mindful that the power plant, the dynamo, the reservoir of all that power is outside each.

Almost all love songs are in the present or the future tense: "I will love you 'til the sands of the desert grow cold…" or "We will raise a family…" or "I'll bake a cake for you to take for all the boys to see.…" Where are the songs about the same lovers ten years after marriage? Was the bungalow built? Was the cake ever baked? The fact is that he who promises an infinite ecstasy of love is lying; he is selling what he does not possess. There is much unhappiness ahead when the flickering, smoldering wax promises the light that belongs to the sun. The ocean is jealous of its depths and will revenge itself in the little stream that promises the forests a fountain of water equal to the sea.

How different is a woman when she recognizes her role as messenger than when she does not.

When she sees herself as a messenger, she is the image of the highest aspiration of the soul. That is her power. But when she refuses to see herself as a messenger of God's love, she arouses the lowest instincts of a man. This is her weakness. A woman, therefore can be either an object of adoration or an object of scorn. Her beauty can evoke the beauty of the angels; but the moment she surrenders her role as courier of the Divine, she can drag man to the depths. How often a man who has led a mediocre, dull or even wicked life is transformed once he comes under the influence of a good woman. It is not that she ministers to his needs or his instincts, but rather that she unveils the invisible; she brings a message of a holier love and lifts a man even from the gutter as the stained drop of water by the power of the sun is converted into a flake of immaculate snow on a mountain top.

The same is true of a man. When he regards love as a trust from the Divine, he is prepared to make any sacrifice for the one he loves; when he denies the instrumental character of love, he becomes an egotist, bent only on his own pleasure.

One loves an ideal before one loves in fact. We have the plan before the accomplishment; the ideal portrait before the sitter; the original before the fulfillment.

In a mysterious way some great invisible hands had molded an ideal. It seems, therefore, that it is less the person one falls in love with than the ideal. It could very well be that the best and most lasting of human loves are not when flesh and blood awaken in us a spark for the first time, but rather when we love first an ideal and then find the ideal in flesh and blood.

Men or women who do not feel nearer to God when they fall in love ought to ask themselves if they are not beasts rather than persons.

Possessing Another

If one asks a young woman who was a college graduate to tell the year in which Shakespeare was born, or the forces that were engaged in the Battle of Waterloo, or who was Socrates, she could answer. But if she is asked what to do when a husband snaps back an answer, or slams a door, she has no ready response. Marriage is about the only lifelong profession in which there is no preparation or novitiate.

Young people say that they are marrying to find happiness, and they really believe that happiness is identified with possessing a partner, just as one might enjoy possessing a beautiful car, or a country house. How pleased one is with a new car! But after six months one does not notice its tail lights or ash trays, all of which were so important the day when it was purchased.

To marry someone with the idea of possessing him or her is to rob that person of the precious endowment of liberty. If that other person is "mine," like a cocktail, then he or she can never make a present of himself or herself. What I possess I can no longer receive as a gift. You cannot receive a gift of ten dollars if you already have it in your pocket and you own it. The whole meaning of the union breaks down. The very word, "conjugal," means "with a yoke" — "*con jugum*." It is not a dead yoke but a living relationship and an adventure in constant development. There is such a thing as "wave length" in which there is a kind of an accord reached between two persons. This wave length accord is not just a few minutes a day, but for life.

At first the tempests of sexual encounter, its stormy concentration, create the illusion of harmony. But later on there is a realization that the other person is never completely possessed. The basic reason is: the other person belongs to God. This ultimate region is inaccessible. As Helmut Thielicke put it: "Because of the other person's 'alien dignity,' he always retains an ultimate remainder of his own being, which I must respect even in the most intimate and loving encounters as something that is withheld from me and which I dare not lay hands on even in the extreme of ecstasy."

The "hang-over" of all functional love which ignores the dignity of the person is a reminder that flaming torches are not put into hands to burn a city, but to illuminate it. Husbands and wives are not torch-throwers to leave charred ruins, but protectors of great possessions whose title rests in the hands of God.

This hunger and thirst for possession and being possessed ultimately reaches a stage where there is a feeling of being alone together. One realizes the impossibility of uniting two beings. There is a barrier to total possession. Even after the thrill of the capture, there is the deep sense of not having the prey.

To marry someone
with the idea of possessing him or her
is to rob that person of. . . liberty.

Parents and Children

Just as painting is learned best from the great artists, music from its masters, and literature from its inspired poets and dramatists, so too the art of parenthood is best learned from those who have raised good children.

H. Bushnell was once asked, "After all, must not our children answer for themselves?" He responded: "This very often amounts to a negation of the responsibilities of the parental office." Such parents subside into a habit of negligence, like the ostrich. The burden of a father and mother toward children is not diminished, but increased by the personal liberty of the children. It would be far less cruel to be negligent of their bodily wants, for the body will maintain its growth, even when poorly clad and fed upon the coarsest fare, but the mind or soul, born to greater perils than weather, waits to be led into choices and tastes, and finally into habits that are to be its character for eternity.

Some parents are timid about the moral and the spiritual training of their children because of their own failure to be either. A celebrated economist, Le Play, once wrote: "Until I can say grace at meals without astonishing any of my guests, I will not believe that I have done enough for the return of good habits." René Bazin relates how edified he was while visiting in the north of France to observe how the family of an industrialist had said grace faithfully before meals "assigning each child a day to lead."

Recently a New York taxicab driver told me that his eighteen-year-old son would not obey him, nor would he study. He said that he remembered when he went to a Jewish school as a boy, he came home one day and told his father: "The Rabbi slapped me for no reason whatever." The taxi driver recalled that his father told him: "The Rabbi punished you, either because you were disobedient, or because you did not study your lessons, or because you were paying no attention. For that lie, I shall give you a spanking. And I want you to remember that there is a close relationship between the place where you were spanked and the brain." The taxi driver said that he has not lied since.

Another mother, ever conscious of the training of her children for life, gave each of them a watch at the age of twelve. On each she inscribed the words: "May all the hours of your life to the very last, mark the good you do. May you never have to blush for one of them." At that early age she trained them to offer sacrifices to bring blessings on their future homes: "Offer that up for the one whom you will one day marry." Chesterton once said that education is entirely confided to women until a time in life when education becomes rather useless, "for a child is not sent to school to be instructed until it is too late to teach him anything."

Youth

Our contemporary world knows two false views concerning the training of youth: one is an error prevalent in the Western world; the other is an error prevalent in the Communist world. The error of the Western world is that of "emancipation"; the error of Communism is that of force and violence.

Youth is badly trained when emancipation is understood as freedom from control of the teacher, freedom from correction, freedom from restraint, freedom from obedience, freedom from the compelling force of an ideal, freedom from the limitation of law, freedom from homework, freedom from home and freedom from work. In these cases, emancipation becomes identified with lawlessness and freedom with tyranny. Progress, instead of being understood as working toward an ideal, is interpreted as merely a motion. No care is taken as to where youth is going; the important point is that he be on his way. He may, under such a system, become as little green apples, separated from the tree with no roots in the earth, and no branches pointing to the heaven, devoid of tradition on one hand and supreme ideals on the other. When duties to the community and high moral purposes are gone, youth begins to acquire a false value in itself, like an immature plant that is uprooted from the earth. It is then the elders expect youth to create what they themselves have lost.

As the Western world gives up discipline and restraint, Communism picks them up and utilizes them for the sake of the totalitarian state. The workings of Communism on youth take contradictory positions, depending upon whether or not a country has been completely communized. Communist infiltration begins in a democracy by stressing, even more than certain false teachers in democracy, that there is no distinction between right and wrong, virtue and vice. Communists add to this the false theory that there is no such thing as personal guilt; there is only social guilt, which generally is private property or what they call "capitalism." The Communists will even go so far as to incite immorality and addiction to dope in order to intensify the change from liberty into license. In this stage, youth is encouraged to do everything in the name of "freedom" to repudiate their elders and superiors as belonging to an old order, and to live without discipline, correction or rule.

When the Communists, however, take over a country, then their attitude completely changes. Youth is now subjected to a discipline of iron. Youth must surrender its will, its liberty, its opinions and its personalities, in order to establish a revolutionary society. Sacrifice and self-surrender, self-discipline and asceticism now become the pattern of Communist training. Youths are asked to renounce family, friends, thoughts and even themselves. As one Communist youth booklet put it: "If you seek your personal perfection, you deceive yourself. There is but one commandment: Obey the Party."

The error of the Western world is to train youth in love without discipline, which is softness. The Communist error is to train youth in discipline without love, which is hardness. The Golden Mean, or the correct principle of youth training, is freedom through discipline. As a garden is cultivated only by pulling up the weeds, as a colt is broken for service only through the training of the horseman, as atomic energy is utilized for industry rather than for the bombing of a city, so too youth is trained through discipline to realize the glorious freedom of the Children of God.

A Teenager Talks on Responsibility

"You say we have no responsibility, Mom and Pop. You are the product of progressive education; we are the by-product. You were brought up in a progressive school under the influence of John Dewey. He was America's great 'emancipator' in the sense that he emancipated your generation from any subservience either to Church or State. You were taught that there is no obligation to anything except society and that you were not to submit to authority. You were told you had no responsibility except to democracy.

> *. . .all we are doing actually*
> *is eating the fruit of the tree*
> *which you planted.*

"The difference between your generation and mine is this: you were taught there was no responsibility except to society, but you did not practice it. We practice it, and we are called delinquents. You lived in a world of theory; we live in a world of practice, and all we are doing actually is eating the fruit of the tree which you planted.

"Because you were raised in a spirit which denied responsibilities, you began shifting the burden of responsibility to the school and told the teachers that they were responsible for us. But they, too, were trained for the most part the same way as you. You were taught that everything is justifiable and that there is to be no discipline. It was said that everyone must practice self-expression. The child who smeared paint on a canvas was called an artist, as much as any other child who knew something about painting. Ungrammatical idioms were permitted because they were so expressive and one was not to correct a child lest he should feel inferior.

"What was omitted from your education was experience, reasoned demonstrations, the value of prohibitions such as 'Stay away from that fire,' or 'Don't run across the street in crowded traffic.'

"You just thought it was an interesting theory to be told: 'Always do what you want to do.'

"What are the results of this denial of responsibility? There is no one to whom we owe anything. We do not owe anything to God, because we may not mention His Name in school. We do not owe it to society, because society is as mixed up as we are. We thought we owed it to you, but you shifted the blame to the school. So, what do we do? We have to have some standard, and we have taken a smaller society than the nation — namely, our gang, our group of friends, our fellow teenagers.

"There is, therefore, no standard outside of ourselves; no one to whom we are responsible except to ourselves. It just happens to be a smaller society than Dewey's.

"A survey made at Purdue University revealed that fifty-one percent of us teenagers did everything to please either our friends or our gang. So instead of conforming to the Com-

mandments, as did our forefathers, we have our own commandment. That is why we dress alike, we talk alike. That is why
we pretend to like the same kind of music and have the same
heroes. We have to have some sense of responsibility. Where
else can we go except to ourselves?"

A Teenager Talks on Authority

"What I have to say to you now, Mom and Pop, is something rather hard, but it just has to be said: you seem to forget that we cannot have any respect for your commands unless we have respect for you.

"We are constantly being told that we are opposed to authority. We are not opposed to authority; we are opposed only to those who administer it without practicing it. Our love for you does not depend on whether you give us everything we *want*, but because you possess those qualities which command respect.

"If Mickey Mantle told any boy in the school how to hold a baseball bat, the boy from that time on would hold it that way, because of the respect that he has for him in the field of sports. If any celebrated actress told us how to walk onto a stage in our high school play, we would follow that advice every time we walked on a stage. You tell us we ought to obey you. But whom do you obey? Whom do you represent? From whom do you get your authority?

"I asked one of the kids in the class if he ever got an answer to that question, and he said: 'Yes, my parents said that they were baby-sitters for God.' Well, that makes sense.

"If authority comes from God, then in obeying you, I am obeying Him.

"Pop, you tell me not to drink, but you are drunk once a month. Mom, you tell me not to smoke cigarettes, but I heard you say once that you started when you were nine. You told me to keep my word and be true to friends, but do you know that one out of every four in this block is divorced? You tell me I should have religion, but do you ever go to church? Some kids in our class say they have grace before meals and prayers every night. We would feel awkward if we did that.

"We teenagers are smarter than you think. I heard some sophomore the other day say that his parents are seeking social status through their popularity.

"I notice that whenever a teacher lacks any value, he fails to command respect. Disobedience in a class increases. Juvenile delinquency is in direct ratio and proportion to the decline of moral values among parents. Every defect in character is a defect in obedience. Do you remember our doctor told us the other day that he received a telephone call from the mother of one in my class saying: 'My daughter is running around with boys and I wish you would do something about it. She is out until three or four o'clock every morning. I am afraid she will get pregnant and disgrace us all.'

"Another mother received a phone call from a teacher who said that her child had been taking money out of her purse. The mother said: 'I am ashamed of you. Why couldn't you have stolen the money out of *my* purse?' Evidently there is no such thing as stealing being wrong, or unchastity being wrong. It is hard for us teenagers to have any respect for parents like that.

"The last thing I have to say about this is that there have been moments when I have been so proud of both of you because of what you were and what you are. I always, in those moments, found it very easy to obey. I analyzed myself and found out that I never want to hurt anyone I love.

"It reminds me that we stopped in a hotel once in St. Louis and I found a Bible there, and I opened it and read the passage where Jesus gave authority to Peter to feed His lambs and feed His sheep. I noticed that each time He preceded it by love — 'Do you love Me?' Where there is love, there is obedience."

A Message to Youth

Education in the United States has ceased to be an intellectual privilege, and has become a social necessity. This has resulted in the assumption that the only kind of learning is book learning, but not all youths are suited for book learning. Many an adolescent does not wish to go to school, certainly not to high school. Society is not caring for these people adequately. It makes laws against child labor, but once they have dropped out of school, it makes it impossible for them to find any labor at all. There is a gap between the moment when the boy drops out of school and the point where the economic order takes him in. Would it not be well to establish in this country apprentice villages, such as exist in Austria, for job training? Could not unions with their tremendous capital, and management with their great profits, combine to form apprentice schools, alongside of industries, training youth not only for that particular industry, but for crafts and sciences in general? Social workers who are wont to excuse juvenile delinquency are not wrestling with the problem, which is to give them a mission and a purpose, an affirmation of their personality, a sense of belonging to society and of having a meaningful career.

A second remedy is not just mission, but vision. Here,

one touches the Beatitude "Blessed are the clean of heart for they shall see God." There is an intimate relationship between purity and the vision of perfect happiness. Purity prepares for a double vision: one, intellectual; the other, spiritual. Intellectual vision is perfected by keeping biological energies intact until Providence prepares the one who shall receive them. Erotic energy, when kept continent is not wasted, but is transformed. The same energy, for example, that a businessman spends in making money could also make him a saint. The energy of a criminal could help remake society. The biological energy that is treasured goes into the intellect and into the making of character. A negative evidence of this is that the youth who falls into erotic excesses will also fall down in his studies. When all of the honeyed treasures of his body are spent, there is no new intellectual life to show. Of the Knights of the Round Table, Sir Galahad was the one who had the strength of ten because his heart was pure. While all the Knights sought to see the Holy Grail, that vision was given to this pure-hearted Knight, "For such as thou art is the vision, not for these."

There is also the relationship between purity and faith. The want of faith in the modern world is not due to the fact that men are not given reasons for faith; rather the reason comes from want of proper conduct. The impure may see all — except God, and that is why in the end they will see nothing. Sin will not cheat a man out of the fragrance of the rose, but it will cheat him out of the sweeter soul-fragrance of the Divine, which is folded in every petal.

After mission and vision, comes nonconformism. It used to be some generations ago, that the honest, the monogamous, the pure were on the reservation, while the pornographic, the adulterers and the divorced were off it. Today, it is almost the reverse. That is why a special kind of non-conformism is necessary today — namely, a resistance on the part of the good to the evil tide that would sweep away culture and national security.

Socialists used to hold that economic wealth absorbs the have-nots, so that the rich become richer and the poor become poorer. Today, there is another kind of absorption which is even more dangerous, and that is the quantitative absorbing the qualitative. History decays in favor of the masses or those who do nothing but follow. Daring to be a "square" means that honest and decent youths will not fit in with the beatniks and the chiselers, the sharpshooters and the perverts. A dead body floats downstream. It takes a live body to resist it. The rotten apple is pleasant to the worm, but not to the palate of a man.

The rebirth of youth will come from youth itself. If the legal profession ever became corrupt, it would not be bettered by doctors giving them lectures, but by honest lawyers regenerating their profession from within. So it is with youth. Social workers, courts and even the clergy will only be the indirect agents for remaking a creative youth. As the Communists lay hold of a few corrupt individuals to corrupt the mass, so the leaders of youth will find among them a vast army who are specially competent in the way of leadership, who refuse to bend the knee to false gods, and who will take away the reservations from the punks and give it to the young who will be "squares" like Lincoln, Washington and other great Americans.

Mystery

Every human being at his birth has everything to learn. His mind is a kind of blank slate on which truths can be written. How much he will learn will depend upon: (1) how clean he keeps his slate, and (2) the nobility and wisdom of his teachers.

The cleanliness of the slate is dependent upon the way he lives. It is too often assumed that ignorance is due solely to a want of learning. Actually, an evil life prevents the accumulation of wisdom. No bank robber wants to have a searchlight turned upon him as he rifles a safe. In an equal way, no one who is leading an immoral life wants to have the light of moral truth shining upon his foulness. That is why Our Blessed Lord said of many: "You will not come to Me because your lives are evil."

The second condition of learning depends upon the nobility and wisdom of the teachers. These teachers exist on three levels: man may learn from nature alone, which makes him a scientist; or from men, which makes him a humanist; or he may learn from God, Who alone can give him wisdom.

Almost all are willing to learn, either from the book of nature or from the lips of men, but many are unwilling to accept the revelation of God. This is because what God reveals very often transcends both the power of nature and the learning of men. For that reason, it is called a "mystery." A mystery does not mean an idea which is opposed to reason, but one which transcends reason. Mystery is like a telescope to the eye: the instrument does not destroy vision, but rather opens it to new worlds hitherto unrevealed. A proud man might ask why should he believe that there is anything else in the world to see or know, except that which he touches or sees. Such an egotistic view precludes the knowledge of other worlds.

G.K. Chesterton once said that God has put a tremendous mystery in nature itself, and that is the sun. In the light of that one thing, which we cannot see because of its brightness, everything else is made clear. Likewise, though we cannot comprehend the nature of God completely in this life, nevertheless, in the light of the truths which He reveals, everything else is made clear, such as the mystery of pain, suffering, death, life and birth. But we can see the moon and we can see things under the moon, from which Chesterton wisely deduces: "But the moon is the mother of lunatics."

There are two kinds of wisdom: the wisdom of the flesh and the wisdom which God gives. One is very often opposed to the other. The first would say: "This is the only life there is; therefore, we should get all we can out of it." The other sees that this life is a kind of scaffolding up through which we climb to eternal happiness. But this Divine Wisdom comes only to those who have qualifications for receiving it, and as was pointed out above, one of the first conditions is good behavior. As Our Blessed Lord said: "If any man will do My Will, he will know My doctrine."

Vices produce a hardened spiritual feeling which hinders

understanding. Men do not understand what they do not like or what would demand a change in their lives. All the training of the university will not make certain persons mathematicians. If a man does not love truth and honesty, he cannot be made truthful and honest by expounding the definitions of these virtues. One must begin by creating within him conduct along the lines of these virtues. Then he can be taught the meaning of truth and honesty. One can cure a bad passion only by producing a good one; one can expel an evil affection only by the Spirit of God. Here is the answer to the question of why some people who are otherwise learned do not attain to the wisdom which is revealed by God.

Pilate was a philosopher and belonged to the school of the pragmatists. He talked with Our Lord about His Kingdom and about truth, but Pilate's corrupt selfishness and his political interests permitted him to sentence Innocence to the Cross. There was moral blindness in close conjunction with philosophical intelligence. This higher wisdom is faith, and faith is not a blind willingness to believe that something will happen. Faith is the acceptance of a truth on the authority of God revealing it, and this is the wisdom which sometimes children possess, and learned men lack. That is why Divine Wisdom said that only as we became like little children, could we enter the Kingdom of Heaven.

Turning
from the Road
of Evil Intent

Forgiveness meets us more than halfway.
The kiss of welcome is extended
before one word of penitence or request
had been spoken.

Why Am I Tempted?

The question is not why do we sin, because there is a distinction between temptation and sin. Temptation is merely a solicitation, an invitation, a suggestion to do wrong. Sin is the voluntary doing of that wrong thing. Scripture says, "Blessed is the man who suffers temptation." In this context, temptation means trial. The sixth petition of the Lord's Prayer, "Lead us not into temptation," is a petition to escape trials which we cannot master.

When Scripture states that God tempted Abraham, it merely means God tried Abraham's faith as a goldsmith tries gold in the fire; there is a world of difference between God trying His people and inciting their corruption.

Coming more precisely to the subject of temptation, here are a few basic principles:

I. Temptation comes from the duality or complexity of our nature. We are not simple creatures like crystals, but rather a compound of body and soul, matter and spirit. The human personality is like a driver in a chariot, as Plato suggested. Before him are two headstrong steeds: one is the animal urge with us, and the other the spirit. The charioteer, or the drive, has great difficulty to get both steeds headed in the same direction.

Though modern psychology has done much to develop the nature of this tension, it must not be thought that the tension inside man was not known in the past. The greatest of Greek dramatists, Sophocles, wrote of the great primeval disharmony that it was "grave with age and infected all men." Ovid, the Latin poet, wrote: "I see and approve the better things of life, but the worse things in life I follow."

Every human being in the world can bear witness to the civil war which goes on inside his being. Good people sometimes act like bad people; very bad people, in certain circumstances, will act like good people. Goethe regretted that God had made him only one man. There was enough material in him for both a saint and a villain.

2. It must not be thought that the origin of temptation is solely to be sought in the individual human personality. If the origin were wholly within the person, it is conceivable that some would be without temptation; but there is no one in the world who is not tempted — absolutely no one. The nature of the temptation may vary one from another, and they may even vary with age. Confucius divided temptations into three different stages of human life: in youth man is tempted to lust, in middle age to pride and power, and in old age to avarice or greed. No one tells the full story of temptation by seeking its origin in a grandfather or a grandmother, or too much love for a father or too little love for a mother, crowded tenements, low calorie diet or insufficient education.

3. The true origin of the conflict is not to be found in the individual exclusively but in human nature. This assumes there is a difference between "nature" and "person." Nature answers to the question, "What is it?" A person answers to

the question, "Who is it?" A pencil is not a person. An atom is not a person. John Jones is a person. Something has happened to disturb the original human nature so that it is now neither an angel nor a devil. Human nature is not intrinsically corrupt (as some theologians claimed 400 years ago); nor is it intrinsically divine (as philosophers began saying fifty years ago). Rather, human nature has aspirations for good which it sometimes finds impossible to realize completely by itself; at the same time, human nature has inclinations to evil which solicit it away from these ideas.

It is like a man who is down a well of his own stupidity. He knows that he ought not to be there, but he cannot get out by himself. Or to change the picture, he is like a clock whose mainspring is broken. He needs to be fixed on the inside, but repairs must be supplied from without. He is a creature who can run well again, but only if Someone outside has the kindness to repair him. This Someone is Christ, the Son of God and the Redeemer of human nature. He came not to teach but to heal the breach caused by false freedom.

Habit, Not Instinct

The difference between a habit and an instinct is that a habit is acquired, whereas an instinct is infused. A duck never has to acquire the instinct to swim, but a man has to develop it. Habit then means not only the facility of doing a thing because one has done it frequently, but it also implies the impulse of the will to do the action. Because of the lack of will, no inanimate creatures ever develop habits. A clock does not go by continued repetition of its movements. But habit is developed by the will. A drunken Rip Van Winkle, in Jefferson's play, excuses himself for every fresh dereliction by saying: "I won't count this time." He may not count it, but it is counted nonetheless. The nerve cells, fibers and the molecules are counting it, registering it and storing it up to be used against him when the next temptation comes. A man becomes a permanent drunkard by separate drinks, and he becomes a permanent saint by separate acts of virtue.

No man becomes bad at once. Evil is not native to the soul; it has to become domesticated. Any evil desire or affection repeatedly acted upon receives less and less attention from the conscience, until at last it almost becomes automatic, like reaching for a cigarette after one has acquired the habit. At first, an act of vice requires an effort and is speedily followed by regret. This voice of conscience is more and more diminished after the evil deed is multiplied.

A man may eventually reach a point where he has a memory of the knowledge of morality, as well as the memory that it exercised over his conduct at one time. But the power of moral cause is gone, though he may falsely justify himself by calling moral precepts superstitions or the relic of a bygone age or a mark of his immaturity.

It would seem that Our Blessed Lord did not recommend a gradual breaking of a habit, but immediate: "If your eye causes you to sin, tear it out and throw it away. It is better for you to enter into life with one eye than with two eyes to be thrown into fiery Gehenna." He did not actually mean a physical plucking out of the eye, but a complete break with the evil habit. A short time ago a drunk stopped me on the street and said: "I am a bum; I have no job and I drink too much. What would you recommend?" I said to him: "The first thing that you must do is to want to be sober and decent and hardworking." He said: "Oh, no. That is too hard." Though Dr. Jekyll made up his mind to have done with the hateful life he carried on in the form of Mr. Hyde, he did not destroy the cup and the liquid which enabled him to transform himself into a safe disguise. It is the destruction of the cup and the will to be better which is the condition of breaking the evil habit.

J. Arthur Thomson well emphasized this necessity of suppressing the animal in us in order to encourage the angel: "Man often seems like a creature whose wings have been smirched with oil or bedraggled with mud, so that it cannot fly.... There are gratuitous handicaps which can be got rid of, so as to leave the developing human spirit to go forth with a new freedom on this quest after adventures in the kingdom of the spirit."

So many say it is their weak wills which keep them from rising. It is not just the will that is weak; it is rather the refusal to accept the truth that the will has the power to rise, particularly when there is a power supplied from the outside, namely, the power of grace. In breaking evil habits, man does not act alone; he acts in conjunction with help from God, if he but claims it. The wise old Pythagoras used to say: "Choose that course of action which is best, and custom will soon render it the most agreeable." If we kept a tiger alive and expect to manage him, the best thing to do is to feed him; but if we desire to kill him, the only thing to do is to stop his food at once and for a little while he will roar and tear, but will soon grow weak.

Breakdown of Honesty

Many problems which never before entered the conscience or were discussed by an honest man are now openly debated, such as how much can one pad an expense account without being caught? Should one build obsolescence into products so that they will have to be repurchased every few years or every few months? Should boxes of foodstuffs be made larger and contents smaller?

How such questions in a culture which is more and more disregarding honesty will be answered was made evident in a national reaction to a Los Angeles Negro a few years ago. Mr. Douglas Johnson is a middle-aged Negro janitor, whose story was written up in *Life* magazine. An armored car passing ahead of him accidentally dropped a sack through an open door. The sack contained $240,000 in bills of ten and twenty dollars. Mr. Johnson and his wife Helen returned the money to the owners and received a $10,000 reward. This type of story was the one which always started the Horatio Alger books for boys a few decades ago. But Douglas Johnson, instead of receiving praise, was stunned by the abuse. Motorists passed by his house, hooted at him, his wife and his children, called them "stupid," sent letters telling what he could have done with the money. One person said: "If I got it, I would still be driving." Another recommended that the hot money be given to gamblers at Las Vegas who would accept it for a discount. Others suggested going to Mexico. Others suggested spending the money on the track. Still others abused them, saying they were a disgrace to the colored race. Mr. Johnson was ridiculed at work; his children were abused in school. One of them was given a knife and told to go home and cut his father's throat. It ultimately became necessary for the Johnsons to move from their neighborhood to escape further abuse.

After the incident was given some newspaper publicity, then honest people came forward and defended Mr. Johnson. Letters poured in from other parts of the world — from Greece, Ghana, Arabia, Italy, some just bearing the inscription: "The Honest Janitor." Mr. Johnson said: "Returning that money wasn't as big a thing as people seem to think. It didn't have to be that much money. I would have given back any amount I found. It was the normal and the right thing to do."

What reasons may be given for the breakdown of honesty in American life? These reasons immediately come to mind:

I. An affluent and rich culture such as our own soon begins to judge characters by what they have, rather than by what they are. Once having becomes the test of status, there follows the desire to have more and more. A neurotic competitiveness sets in and it is not long until one begins to cut corners to make oneself the top man on the totem pole.

2. Another reason for the dishonesty is to be found in the so-called ethics of our day. Instead of bringing to life a few principles, the tendency today is to build an ethics to suit the way one lives. It used to be that men were kept honest because

they based their lives on the principle: "If I were dishonest, I could not live with myself." Conscience demanded that they keep faith with the moral law within. This gave way to a second and weaker principle, namely: "I could not be dishonest, for otherwise I could not live with my neighbor." Here there was a kind of a fear of social retribution. Both of these are passing out of existence. With the growing dishonesty and the attempt to make the head fit the cap, the new principle is: "Anything is all right, provided you do not get caught or if you can get away with it."

Guilt

George Bernard Shaw once said that modern man is too busy to think about his sins. But though one denies he is personally sinful, yet personal guilt does have social effects.

If there were no guilt, one would not be either so anxious to deny it or so passionately zealous to seek out companionship like unto oneself. That is why communities of guilty people spring up, such as dope peddlers, robbers, perverts and degenerates.

Another effect is the desire to seduce others and tar them with the same brush. The impure cannot stand the sight of the pure; hence, the ridicule of virtue with a solicitation to evil. Hence, in the story of the origin of sin, Eve seeks out the companionship of Adam. The coalition made possible first to blame one another and then finally to blame God for their condition.

There is nothing new in the world. There are only the same old things happening to new people. When, in the beginning, the first man and woman started "passing the buck," trying to hide their shame with withering fig leaves, even nature arose in rebellion against them: there was heard the Voice of God calling, "Man, where are you?" The "you" takes the problem out of the realm of psychology, biology and economics and puts it squarely in the person himself. David could live for months under the illusion that he was justified in sending Uriah into the front line of battle to be killed, but the real reason was that he wanted to take the wife of Uriah to himself. Then the prophet Nathan appeared to him and said, "David, you are the man."

God calls, however, not to condemn but to heal. But cowardly escapism and false self-defenses keep such lonely hearts from healing.

Paul became normal when he said: "I persecuted and killed Your disciples." Every man reaches a degree of normalcy when he can say, "I refused to give You a cup of water when You were thirsty and I nailed a hand to the beam of the cross." The game of "passing the buck" ends when the person is brave enough to come from behind the bushes, be honest with himself and say: "I am the man."

The evasion of responsibility sometimes has a literary expression. One form of this is the false compassion of our modern day which is extended to the guilty rather than to the suffering. "Sob sisters" are found in abundance for the juvenile delinquents who murdered an eighty-year-old woman, or for the movie actor who, under the influence of dope, ran over a child, and for the head of a ring of professional prostitutes. It is guilt which subconsciously makes them do this, for by condoning guilt and even praising it in others they seem to relieve themselves of the unbearable repartee of their own conscience.

Another literary effect is to affirm that since men are no longer living according to traditional morality, therefore we must have a new morality. It is like saying that because dishonesty becomes common among taxpayers, we should no longer have an accounting by the Income Tax Bureau, or because more motorists are driving through the red lights and killing pedestrians, therefore we must put in pink lights. It might be better to stop identifying "progress" with the breaking of law and to revert to the common sense idea that no one is so close to happiness as he who knows he is guilty but pardonable.

Power

The misuse of power is the most common of modern sins. As Lord Acton put it: "All power corrupts; absolute power corrupts absolutely." The ancient political power ruled only over the bodies of men; the modern political power of Communism rules not only bodies, but minds. The old colonialism was of land; the new colonialism is of the spirit. The latter is cruel not only in its use of power, but it often provokes in the hearts of those who are subject to it a longing for power, in order that cruelty may be paid back in kind.

The opposite of power is gentleness, which is best understood in the background of strength; hence, a gentleman is not one who obtrudes his wisdom on the ignorant, nor flaunts his money in the slums of the poor. Rather, he is patient with the slow to understand, tender to the weak, generous to the needy. Gentleness is never weakness, but power clothed in sympathy, as the Gentle Christ was the Omnipotence of God wrapped in swaddling bands.

The great wonder of the Life of Christ is really not His miracles; it is His restraint of power. Being God in the form of Man, He could have turned nails into rosebuds, a crown of thorns into a garland of roses, His Cross into a throne of glory and His Blood into royal purple. At any one moment, He might have breathed His enemies from the face of the earth; but to have all of this Divine Power and never to show it, even under the challenge: "Come down from the Cross," was the highest manifestation of Divine Gentleness.

The weak man is the impulsive man. The quick answer used like a rapier is not a sign of intelligence, but of egotism and pride. About the only time Our Lord used His Power and then sheathed it was in the Garden, when the soldiers came to arrest Him. "Who are you looking for?" He asked. When they said, "Jesus of Nazareth" they all fell to the ground helpless. He then restored their power and gave them the strength to crucify Him, He reserving the ultimate Power to rise from the dead.

Anyone who looks deeply into his own life must marvel at the longsuffering of God in the face of those who would silence prayers to Him in a school, or who blot His Friends from the face of the earth. Divine Power is veiled in gentleness, because its purpose is not to destroy but to save. "The broken reed He will not crush, and the burning flax He will not extinguish." No one ever receives all the stripes he deserves nor all the punishment his iniquities merit. Nor is this royal clemency an indifference to justice and righteousness, but a forbearance that, with a little digging and fertilizing, the tardy tree may grow.

It will always be found that those men with power who are most gentle are always those who are hardest on themselves. He who is not at war with himself is at war with his fellow man. The power that loves self is always cruel, but power that tempers its ego by love is always gentle.

James and John would have brought down fire from heaven

to destroy the Samaritans who would not give the Lord welcome; but in His gentleness, He rebuked them and told them that they knew not what manner of men they were. The issue would not be forced then. He would give the people time to repent as He set out for another village.

> *This heart hath walls that anger never shook;*
> *But love shall break and take it with a look.*

Causes of Violence

The first reason for violence is hatred of virtue because of a bad conscience. This hatred of goodness expresses itself in violence. A boy in a gang who refuses to break school windows will invariably be taunted and ridiculed by the rest of the gang. His refusal to destroy property is an indirect condemnation of their destructiveness. A faithless husband running around with other women will often either beat his wife or torture her mentally because her very fidelity is to him a rebuke. She becomes his conscience and placards before his mind his adultery. To justify his own filth, he must throw mud. The young woman in a college dormitory who refuses to take part in the orgiastic abandon of her fellow students will be ridiculed for her virginity.

No one who does wrong is comfortable in that wrong, unless everyone else is dragged down to his level. This is one of the reasons why teenagers whose excessive drinking and late hours are condemned by their parents will always say the parents are "old-fashioned"; they will seek out a group or a gang which will give their misconduct approval. As an individual descends the moral ladder into a decay, he will always seek that level which will give to his dishonesty or his mugging or immorality a stamp of approval, and thus ease his conscience.

This hatred of virtue is so ingrained in weak and fallen human nature that it is easy to predict what will happen to those who retain decency and morality. Suppose there came to this earth someone whose virtue was perfect, whose kindness to the poor and to the afflicted was without limits, whose compassion to the hungry made him hungry, whose oneness with the wounded made him feel their wounds, and who spurned all hypocrisy and short cuts to popularity by a denial of self-discipline — would not all those who fell below that line hate and despise him? If his goodness were perfect, he would be crucified. And this is the ultimate explanation of the Crucifixion of Christ.

The world has little use for two extremes: the very wicked who disturb society too much and the very good or saintly. That is why thieves were crucified on either side of Our Lord because they disturbed the false peace of affluent possessions, and why in their midst was crucified Supreme Goodness. It is the mediocre who survive — those who find in one another an approving pat on the back for every moral declension.

Another reason for violence is the need of punishment. Everyone who steals knows that it is dishonest and the object stolen should be returned to the rightful owner. The broken window should be paid for; the automobile deliberately smashed should be repaired.

Conscience not only tells us what is wrong, but it also tells us that we deserve punishment for what is wrong. By repeated neglects of conscience one can deaden its voice and for the moment feel no consequences, as David did not feel the guilt of murder and adultery until almost a year after the crime. But the need of punishment remains not in the conscious mind, but in the unconscious mind. Because reparation for the wrong does not come out normally, it then begins to come out abnormally. A tube of toothpaste if squeezed with the cap on will break out in an unexpected place. This explains the curious complexes that arise in human nature, such as the excessive washing of hands which is an external symbol of the need of washing one's own soul.

So it is with punishment. The judgment which we should bring to ourselves and which should condemn ourselves for wrong is projected to others. This probably is the psychological reason for the love of violence and horror movies, television shows and stories in our contemporary civilization. We must see punishment; we must see a reparation; we must see justice done. But instead of applying it to ourselves, we take a fiendish delight in seeing others suffering. Expiation is done not by self but by others. The criminal is punished. The horrors of conscience are projected to the horrors on the screen. Instead of confessing their own guilt and doing penance, people deny their own guilt and accept the garroting, machine-gunning and bayoneting of others as a substitute for the punishment which in their own hearts they know they justly deserve.

The first reason for violence
is hatred of virtue
because of a bad conscience.

Turning Violence into Mercy

Love of violence is one of the most dangerous symptoms of our civilization. The fondness of seeing someone struck or blood shed or a life taken betokens some deep and ingrained hatred in the heart of man. Is there any power of influence capable of removing this passion for cruelty and transmuting it into compassion and mercy? Perhaps the answer is to be found in the story of one of the most famous jailers of all history. He lived in the city of Philippi, named after the father of Alexander the Great. There the battle between Brutus and Anthony was fought, after which — chagrined by his defeat — Brutus who had slain the great Caesar slew himself. It was in this city, too, that Christianity was first preached to all Europe by Paul and Silas.

These two apostles were arrested by three Roman authorities because a conversion had despoiled the revenue of some dishonest men. They were dragged into the forum, where the magistrates ordered them scourged "without measure." The Jewish law limited scourging to forty stripes save one. But here the jailer bared their backs upon which were rained heavy blows causing the blood to spurt at every stroke. The jailer then led them to the deepest and most foul-smelling den, and thrust their feet into stocks.

In contrast to the gory violence of the jailer, the apostles Paul and Silas, instead of groaning and complaining, began to sing. Never before were such sounds heard in those dreary walls. Fellow criminals awakened at midnight heard not the ravings of agony, but prayer and praise and song.

Then suddenly there came an earthquake. Every door of the prison opened; every man's chains fell off and they stood once again as free men. But the jailer, knowing that he lived in a land of violence and that he too would be subject to it because of their release, drew his sword to kill himself. Paul said: "Do no harm to yourself; we are all here." Then bringing a light, the jailer fell at the feet of Paul and Silas asking: "What must I do to be saved?" Paul told him to believe that belief in Christ the Savior alone would save him. He was converted and with him his whole household. What could not be accomplished by ordinary means was accomplished by a sudden upheaval of nature.

The next scene takes us to the house of the once violent man. He who had laid whips to the backs of Paul and Silas now washes their wounds and applies healing balm. The desire to inflict pain had now become the passion to relieve it. And what wrought the transformation was no soft word about humanity, but the awakening in the once cruel heart of his relation to the unseen world. This alone changed his attitudes toward the seen world.

The question he asked was: "What must I do to be saved?" He suddenly realized that he as a "yonder-minded being, and embodied hereafter" and that violence was putting him out of that orbit. When that question was answered by Paul, mercy began to flow. The jailer used his hands to wash the wounds;

he used his house to entertain Paul and Silas; and he used his larder to feed them. Pity comes from faith; hatred and bloodshed from the want of it. As Basil wrote: "His act of pity was the first sacrifice of thanks he offers for his conversion, a sacrifice as a whole burnt offering, and yet not by fire, but by water kindled and inflamed." His small work done, and colored in the blood of Paul, appears now like a red thread that hung from Rahab's window as a pledge of salvation. St. John Chrysostom tells us that the names of the jailer and his wife were Euodias and Syntiche whom Paul enrolls in the book of life. Violence is due to want of faith, but there is no evidence that faith cannot cure.

The Case for Chastity

[handwritten margin note: What is called repression is really expression]

There is a whispering campaign going on against chastity. The young are told that it is bad to repress themselves; that self-expression is always good. This is really a trick in words because there is never any expression without a repression of some kind. To repress the desire to rob a bank is to express the virtue of honesty; to repress a desire to drink too much alcohol is to express sobriety and good sense.

Other times it is said: "Everybody's doing it," and that "It doesn't make any difference anymore." Morality is not made by numbers. Communism is not right because it succeeds in repressing everyone in China.

One of the great dangers of pre-marital experiences is that it causes conflicts in the boy and the girl. They cannot separate the early experience which gave satisfaction with the later experience of mature, personal and intellectual satisfaction.

And as regards frustration, here is the statement of one woman who had gone through the extra-marital experience and wrote: "Much is talked of the evil of frustration in the case of the woman who denies herself the physical expression of love. In my opinion that vague and generally periodic torment is nothing compared to the frustrations suffered by a woman who seeks happiness in love outside of marriage… it is a trapped, blind-alley feeling that only one who has experienced it can appreciate. The conflict set up as a result of it is keen and distracting and almost from the outset casts its dark shadow over an experience which one had expected to be all light and freedom."

Very often such people are worn out before they are thirty, and have never touched the deeper aspects of happiness. Overstimulated and wrongly stimulated, they cannot later respond to normal marriage relations and the chances of compatibility are poor. Any divorce of the sexual experience from the spiritual experience is bound to create a disturbed mind. As one doctor put it: "Promiscuity makes people lose the greatest experience in life: love."

Pre-marital experience also destroys certain inhibitions in the young which prepares them for infidelity later on in life.

Men and women living in chastity are very well balanced psychologically and physiologically. But there are innumerable cases of men and women living anything but chastely who are tortured by sexual obsessions and psychic conflicts. Continence is in no way damaging to the human being.

A very strong case could be made out also for the fact that those who contain themselves allow their energy to spend itself in another direction. It often does produce creativity, either artistic or literary, and especially in compassion for the poor.

Purity is not something negative, just as pure water is not the absence of dirt. The pure diamond is not merely absence of carbon. Purity is a reverence for a mystery, and the mystery is that of creativeness. God has given to man and woman a terrific power of prolonging creation, of begetting new life. One, therefore, will always be reverent about the use of this power until God determines when it shall be put to work. God is the Master of all circumstances of life and will put into your way, in what would seem the most ordinary way, what is actually His Divine Plan.

An essayist makes this startling statement: "What a sad age this is in which one makes his First Holy Communion to be through with religion, receives his college degree to be through with study, and marries to be through with love."

Purity is not something negative,
just as pure water is not the absence of dirt.

Thorn in the Flesh

It is true that every man has his weakness, and to recognize it is a mark of charity. What we do with that weakness, such as alcoholism, lust or dishonesty, or with our sickness and trial, is a test of character. St. Paul had a "thorn in his flesh." We do not know what it was; there had been many guesses such as blindness, physical disease and constant persecution. The point is that he prayed three times to have it taken away from him, but the Lord refused to do it, saying that He would give him sufficient strength to bear it.

Many battles may go on until a man dies, but he need never become depressed about the battle. Nobody in the world can say he has nothing to do, for he has something to do as long as he has something to overcome. Life puts everyone to a test. In fact, our inner weakness is a greater test than outer circumstances. The crooked branch will not bend in a new curve if it is tied only for a few minutes. The tendency toward egotism and selfishness is not cured by one resolution; the thorn may remain even though we ask that it be taken from us. The answer to prayer is not always in the external removal of some pressure or sorrow, but rather the infusing of a power to sustain it. If a man has a burden on his back, he can be relieved in two ways: either by making light of the burden, or by making the shoulder stronger. The latter is sometimes God's way of dealing with us.

Demosthenes became the great orator because he had a weakness of speech. Would we ever have had the poems of Elizabeth Barrett Browning if her spirit had not overcome the sufferings when her spine was injured by a fall from a horse, when she was kept a prisoner in her father's house until she married, and when, as an invalid, she spent most of her life propped up on a couch by cushions. The sparks of her love poetry came not from one who bemoaned her pain but from one who saw in it all the "shade of God's Hand outstretched caressingly."

Most of us are in prison walls; we would like to do other work than that which is forced upon us. Shall we break under it, complain and rebel, or shall we use the time to the profit of our souls? Circumstances, whatever they be, are occasions for the acceptance and working of Divine Power. St. Paul was stoned at Lystra. A young man stood, looking on with admiration. Paul must have recalled when he was a young man and looked on someone else who was stoned. In any case, that night Paul discovered Timothy, the strong comrade of his labor in later years. No wonder he glorified in his infirmities. God works with broken reeds and burning flax, but not with iron pillars which glory in their strength. With self-conceit, He can do nothing. Power that counts itself power is weakness, and weakness that knows itself to be weakness is strength, for when the ego is emptied, Divine fullness can pour in. When a man is weak, he can become strong with grace. So too, when a man knows he is a sinner, then he has already taken the first step toward righteousness and peace.

Temptations to Goodness

Practically all the nourishment the earth gives to man comes from the top four inches of soil. But in the depths of the earth are hidden gold, diamonds, and other precious things. So it is with persons; we judge through our commerce with them on the surface; the way they *seem* to act, the manner of speech and the ephemeral judgments based on the common hearing of the hourly newscast. As a result, most humans are thought to be very superficial, when the truth is that those who seem to have no depth at all to careless eyes really contain treasures of surpassing worth. What is often interpreted as shallowness in others is really a hiding of tragic forces, which only in great storms are brought to the surface.

A young divorced woman who seemed to be lost in the whirl of fashion took into her home on weekends a young victim of leprosy whom society disdained. I said to her: "I know why I have him in my home; it is because he stands for Christ Who bore in His Body all the sins and leprosy of the world. But why do you have him in your home?" She answered: "For the same reason." One would never have suspected such deep fountains of sympathy and compassion.

What is true of the depths in others is also true of ourselves. It has been said that every atheist is afraid in the dark. Herod, who did not believe in a future life, nevertheless believed that Our Lord was John the Baptist risen from the dead. Communists, who deny religion, talk much about it. There is a buried life in every soul awaiting resurrection. As J. Hunter put it:

> *Yet still, from time to time, vague and forlorn,*
> *From the soul's subterranean depth upborne*
> *As from an infinitely distant land,*
> *Come airs, and floating echoes, and convey*
> *A melancholy into all our day.*
> *A bolt is shot back somewhere in our breast*
> *And a lost pulse of feeling stirs again.*
> *The eye sinks inward, and the heart lies plain.*

In these subconscious depths of the soul come inspirations which are too noble to be of our making; the mud and slime which sink down to our subconscious mind cannot suddenly shoot forth flowers and blossoms. There is some other force from the outside which completely changes the direction of our lives. Traveling in the pathways of triviality, it takes some alien Power from the outside to divert us into the Highway of the King. The old theologians used to call these motivations to goodness, "Actual Graces." A better wording would be temptations to goodness.

Why is it that we practically always use the word "temptation" to imply an inclination to evil? Actually, every soul has more temptations to be good than it does to be evil. And we turn down more temptations to virtue than we do to vice. It is, therefore, quite wrong to think of our subconscious mind as a snake pit of rottenness and corruption. There may be some snakes of our own hatching, but there are many more visitations of the angels or holy inspirations prompting us to realize the potentialities of our being.

The famous Psalm which begins with the words: "Out of the depths have I cried to You, O Lord" is a poetic expression of this truth. There are two kinds of despair: the hellish despair which comes from a man relying solely on his own resources, and the creative despair which makes one cry to God, from Whom saving experiences come. The surface of life seems to say one thing to us, and it often is hopelessness and despair; but the depths cry out to something else that is not of our own making.

Selfishness always rides on the thin ice of the soul, but true peace of mind comes from the fountains of the deep in which there is a cry to connect oneself with the invisible and eternal source of truth and love. If man could ever escape from himself he could escape from God, but even when he lands on the moon he brings himself with him. The pendulum has no sense apart from the clock, nor the carbon without the original, nor the shadow without the light. All escapes are vain, as Francis Thompson found when he wrote: "I fled Him down the nights and down the days… but ever and anon came on the Voice: Lo, naught contents thee who contents not Me."

The Silent Quest

One of the really great needs of our own day is silence. Modern life seems to thrive on a fondness for noise, and by noise is meant not only the staccato barbarism of jazz, but also and principally the excessive desire for that which distracts — love of amusements, constant goings and comings, excitements and thrills, and movement for the mere sake of movement.

What is the reason for this fondness of noise? It is not due to any inherent love of that which is loud, for people generally prefer that which is soft and refined. Rather, the reason is to be found in the great desire on the part of human beings to do the impossible, namely, to escape from themselves. They do not like to be with themselves because their conscience reproves and carries on an unbearable repartee. They do not like to be quiet because the footsteps of the Hound of Heaven, which can be heard in silence, cannot be heard in the din of excitement; they do not like to be silent because God's voice is like a whisper and it cannot be heard in the tumult of the city streets.

These are some of the reasons why the modern world loves noise, and they are all resolvable to this — noise drowns out God's voice and stupefies conscience. Dull indeed are these distractions, but like the clay used by savages to dull the pain of hunger, they stifle in the soul the hunger for the presence of God. The result is that very few people ever know themselves. In fact, they know every one else better than they know themselves.

In order to remedy this, what is needed is less amusing and more musing; a silence; a going apart into the desert of our souls to rest awhile; a solitariness from men and an aloneness with God. A quiet is needed which permits the soul to be sensitive to the whispers of God; a rest from modern maxims and the excuses of new philosophies and the excitements which appeal to the body and disturb the soul. There should be a privacy inspired by the example of Him Who, least of all mankind, needed a preparation of silence for a life of activity, and yet had the greatest of them all; a tranquillity inspired by Him Who in the midst of a busy life spent whole nights on mountaintops in prayer.

Silence is the condition of entering into oneself, which is another way of saying, of finding God. Charles de Foucauld, a soldier of France and a man of dissipation, was brought to the very threshold of sanctity by the silence of the Eastern skies, where stars seem so close that one could almost reach up and pluck them out of the heavens. Foucauld died as a priest, perhaps massacred for his faith by the Muhammadans, and yet he came to Christ through the repose and quiet forced upon him by his life in the French Foreign Legion.

We cannot travel to the quiet of the Oriental skies, but we need not; for silence is not dependent upon a place, but upon a state of mind. It is not based on where we are, but what we are thinking about. It is being alone as far as the world is concerned, even though one is in the very midst of it — an activity by which every faculty of the heart and mind and soul is bent inward, awaiting the voice of God.

Patience

Many evil things are done quickly. Hence the Divine Savior, the night of the Last Supper, said to Judas who was about to betray Him: "What you are going to do, do quickly." Satan on the mount of temptation tried to induce Our Lord to a short cut of saving men, and not by the Cross of Redemption. He promised all the kingdoms of the world "now." The reward for leaving evil in the hearts of men was the immediate delivery of political powers of earth.

Impatience or precipitous hurry is related to pride and to egotism. The annoyance felt at the cold coffee, the late morning newspaper, the delay in the appointment, all betray that the ego is considered that which must be served immediately.

The businessman is always in a hurry; even his pleasures are fast. He does not taste food; he gulps it. He waits not for fruit; he plucks blossoms. About the only patience he has, and it is not true patience, is waiting for the stock market to go higher. This is really not patience, but a haunting quest for "more."

Youth, too, has something of this impatience in its precociousness as regards pleasure. At an early age youth can feel already jaded, among some of life's sensible experiences. There is a lust of finishing life, even before it has begun. That is why there is such a love of speed, for the speed of youth is not to get to a certain point, but to show impatience with life.

Despite the American love of hurry, in the New Testament alone there is a recommendation to patience thirty-three times. Patience is not a passivity, but a strong endurance in the face of seeming defeat and disappointment; it is a refusal to be crushed by the blows of circumstances.

Two of the most famous expressions are: "He who believes, does not hasten," and "In your patience, possess your souls." The possession of the soul describes the state in which a person has full command and undisturbed enjoyment of himself in opposition to outside influences, which disturb and decompose his peace of mind. Vain is wealth and prosperity and even health when unrestrained violence of temper becomes a source of disturbance and vexation. The loud complaint, the querulous temper and the fretful spirit disgrace character and show that the mind is unmanned by misfortunes.

There are many who excuse themselves, saying that if they were in other circumstances they would be much more patient. This is a grave mistake, for it assumes that virtue is a matter of geography and not of moral effort. It makes little difference where we are; it all depends on what we are thinking. What happens to us is not so important as how we react to what happens. Patience is not absence of action. It waits for the right time to act, for the right principles and in the right way.

Patience is not insensibility. It is a result of thought. It is a very active bearing up of oneself under the pressure of calamity. Every man has a soul to save, but this cannot be done except by steadfast loyalty to the highest and the best. Patience then is a submissive waiting, a frame of mind which is willing to wait because it knows Whom it serves, because it is willing to endure in gratitude to Him Who endured all, and also because the soul is worth more than the universe.

Satan on the mount of temptation
tried to induce Our Lord to a short cut of saving men,
and not by the Cross of Redemption.

Salvation

What often passes as religion is nothing but ethics and natural morality. Religion as a Divine force implies something that is non-human; namely, a gift from above which can be accepted or rejected. God in some way enlightens the mind to see a truth that was never seen before; He strengthens the will to do things about it that were never done before, thus setting before us motives which will persuade the will to accept what is freely given. This gift is called grace, because gratis.

The grace of God is like the light of the sun which is outside the window. If the blinds of our will are down, or if the windows are dirty because of our behavior, the light will not come in. Human cooperation is, therefore, essential for the entering into a higher and Diviner life than the merely human. All this is a very mysterious and slow process. In the springtime the fields are arrayed in their beautiful vesture, but one cannot see the power of God raising the sap through root and fibre, along stem and branch, and unfolding each bud and blossom.

So it is with the work of salvation. No angels announced that God has commenced His earthly life. He who, however, begins to be responsive to the gift, immediately sees that there are tremendous obstacles to be surmounted, mountains of pride and self-righteousness to be laid low, prejudices to be swept away. The consideration that God works in the soul leaves it without either excuse for negligence or ground for despondency.

Anyone with psychological insight can see a kind of interaction going on inside of himself. On the one hand, there is the overcoming and the casting out of evil, and on the other, there is the assimilation and unfolding of good. It is like passing from disease to health. There is a joint working of God and man, man being able to do his part because God works, and God's working requires man's cooperation. The food in our stomach will not avail us for health, unless the organism cooperates. We must at least be able to digest it. God can no more become the spiritual life, light and strength of the soul any more than undigested bread can become the staff of life.

Most human beings refuse to allow Divine workings in their soul because it requires a change of behavior. The result is continued mediocrity and ordinariness. Man without the grace of God is like a body without food. What a starving man is, such is man without God. It would be foolish for a starving man to say: "I cannot take any food until I am stronger." How could he expect to be strong without food? One cannot feed on oneself. That is why humanism is insufficient. God is waiting to do His Part; we in secret either cooperate or lose the benefit.

Turning
from the Road
of Conceit

Many are cradled
in the sacred associations of the Church.

Jealousy

Jealousy is unconscious self-condemnation. We hate ourselves for not being as good or perfect as the other person. It is also an unconscious acknowledgment of the superiority of others. As someone has said: "Jealousy is the tribute which mediocrity pays to genius." The jealous person always regards the good qualities of another as stolen from him.

We hate less the evil which happens to us than the good we cannot attain. Perfect Goodness was crucified. Instinctively the jealous persons know the good that others do, but they are jealous because they have not done it themselves; therefore, they seek to nullify it by saying it was no good at all.

The elder son in the Gospel parable, who stayed at home, was jealous of the younger son and began accusing him of wasting his substance on evil women. Our Lord never mentioned this fact in telling what the younger son did. It was an imputation of evil on the part of the elder son. Here are two boys who lost the father's love — one because he was too bad; the other because he was too jealous.

Jealousy can take on all kind of forms. For example: women are jealous of others because they are thinner... girls are jealous of others because they are prettier... students are jealous because they are smarter… businessmen are jealous of others because they make more money.

Jealousy can exist between the owner of a peanut stand and the owner of a newsstand, between garbage men, postmen, wives, truck drivers, ministers, priests and bishops. A little girl is jealous of another girl because she has on a nice white dress. Just as soon as she gets a splash of mud on it, then the jealous one is very happy.

When one woman sees another who is lovelier, she might say: "I would hate to be on her diet," or else, "She must spend six hours getting ready."

People who are jealous of others and make judgments about them are already judging themselves. When we call another person "catty," how do we know that person is "catty" unless we ourselves are familiar with "cattiness"? One of the best ways of overcoming jealousy is by complimenting. One day a reporter asked a star what she thought of another star. She said: "Oh, she's okay, I guess, if you like talent."

One of the best ways of curing jealousy is by praying for the one of whom we are jealous. Another way is to make the quality of this person an occasion for imitation, rather than envy, and thus is increased in some way the welfare of humanity and the glory of God. In the words of St. Paul, "But if you go on biting and devouring one another beware that you are not consumed by one another."

Being Superior

The more real power a person has, the less boasting is needed. The less real power he has, the more he seeks to complement it by boasting. The real athlete very seldom boasts or even speaks of his exploits on the field. Missionaries who have spent two or three years in Communist prisons in China very seldom refer to their tortures, lest their fortitude be praised. Saints never speak of their holiness; that is why it is very difficult to portray a truly religious man on the stage. Directors usually think that he must go around with his hands folded, while assuming pietistic attitudes. The real saint keeps his virtues hidden. But the man who would impress others with his holiness must cultivate a certain tone of voice and even join his fingers in an attitude suggestive of prayerfulness. The man who has a right to boast about anything does not have to boast.

Where power is unreal, boasting is used to give the impression of power. The empty wagon always makes the most noise. A person may boast of the college he attended, by which he seeks to have the college reflect on his knowledge, rather than allowing his knowledge to reflect on the college. Also, he believes that by telling a person where he went to school, one will draw conclusions from the college, rather than from his knowledge or want of it.

There are also people who boast about being self-made men and of possessing wealth. Such boasters always prove that they become rich very much to their own surprise. They usually start conversations by telling how they started as a poor boy, without a cent. The only time they even begin to appreciate poverty is when they begin to be rich. The boasting self-made man always confuses "having" something with "being" something.

Human beings in a modern age which knows no humility, strive for a false superiority, either directly or indirectly. Directly, those who have an undue sense of superiority become the dictator type. They are overbearing, loud, critical and proud, and constantly use the pronoun "I." Vain people like to prove themselves right, especially in arguments. What is important is not the truth of things but their being right. Another form of direct superiority is found in those who seek to attract attention by noise, odd mode of dress and the like.

Indirect quests for superiority manifest themselves in the dreamers. Unable to achieve superiority in real life, they live in a world of fantasy in which they believe themselves superior. A child who gets sick just before examination time may see that he cannot realize his fantasy, and thus he develops sickness. Without pain, he would have been forced to prove the greatness of the smartness of which he boasted. Failure to pass would have meant giving up the pretense.

Those have been examples of pride. Pride is an under estimation and an inordinate esteem of one's own excellence. Externals are made substitutes for the internal. The ego is a shell encasing the real self, and the more entrenched we become in our pride, the harder becomes this shell. Pride is at its peak when man cuts himself off from any relation to God, and thus makes himself god. He elevates his relative character into an absolute, very much like a carbon copy calling itself the original. The pendulum of a clock is free to swing as long as it is attached to the mechanism, but once it becomes detached it is no longer free to swing. Man is free when he has a point of suspension to God. When he alienates himself in a false independence, he eventually grows tired of his false freedom. Eventually he looks around for someone to whom he can give up his freedom, which begins to bore him. The cure is to be found in the revival of that forgotten virtue of humility. Humility is a virtue by which we recognize ourselves as we really are, not as we would like to be in the eyes of the public; not as our press notices say we are, but as we are in the sight of God when we examine our conscience.

Letting Off Steam

Letting off steam is very often a modern way of justifying anger. In an age which refuses to believe in any kind of restraint, ill temper is always justified as a means of avoiding extreme pressure. Anger has a right and a wrong side. It is properly used when it prudently condemns moral wrong, as Our Blessed Lord when He drove the buyers and sellers out of the Temple.

One of the strange cases of ill temper in the Scriptures is that of the elder brother who refused to go into the feast when the prodigal brother returned. Ill temper is sometimes found in an otherwise high moral character. The elder brother was without a doubt a man of principle, although he falsely accused the brother of the sin of which there is no record in fact. It is this very association of ill temper with seeming morality which makes temper appear so harmless. We excuse the partial failure of our character on the grounds of its general success.

What is the basic cause of ill temper? It is egotism and selfishness. Those who are guilty of it do not think that they are selfish. They excuse their outbursts either on the grounds that it is their nature, or because they cannot stand injustice, or some similar fragile excuse. But temper is the bad fruit of selfishness. Sometimes the egotist wants something for himself but cannot get it; he then flies into a rage. Hardly any interval exists between the want and the satisfaction of the want, as in the case of infants who cry for things.

Another form of egotism is the belief that one is not treated with as much respect or honor as he thinks he ought to have, and so he sulks; or he is opposed or contradicted in some purpose of his own and he fumes at the rejection of his wish and refuses to have anything to do with people who will not do exactly what he thinks best. A man of bad temper always cares more for himself than he does for other people.

The modern expression for "letting off steam" in more ethical days was called "losing one's temper." This is a phrase which states the fact exactly: something is lost; it is the incontinence which cannot restrain the ego, the leakiness which cannot hold an impulse in, the weak hand that cannot keep its grasp on the lower nature but lets the chained beast loose to do mischief. Though the bad-tempered man prides himself on his manly spirit, actually he loses some manliness, for anger has a double effect. It clouds the intellect and incapacitates the mind for sound judgment; but it also becomes an agent for disarranging human happiness and the charity which should exist among men.

The finest example of charity where ill temper might have been used is to be found in the novel of Victor Hugo. Jean Valjean had been known for nineteen years as prisoner #5623. Turned away from door to door, he comes to the house of Bishop Myriel. The bishop orders a bedroom for him and gives him a seat at table and bids him stay the night. During the night Valjean walks off with silver dishes. He is later captured by the police and returned to the bishop. The bishop pretends that he had made a present of the silver and asks the thief why he did not take the candlesticks as well, for they also were his. When they were left alone together he says to the thief: "Jean Valjean, my brother, never forget that you have promised to employ this silver which I have given you in becoming an honest man. You belong no more to evil, but to good. I have bought your soul. I reclaim it from black thoughts and the spirit of perdition and give it to God."

Jean Valjean was a changed man through charity. As Froude says of Carlyle, who often was irritable and then later on became conscious of how much he had harmed his wife: "For many years she had left him, when we passed the spot in our walks where she was last seen alive, he would bare his grey head in the wind and rain — his features wrung with unavailing sorrow. Let all this be acknowledged; and let those who know themselves to be without anger for others, freely cast stones at Carlyle."

Loneliness

Dante begins one of his finest poems with: "At the mid point of my life I came to the dark wood." By the dark wood, Dante meant that moment in middle age when one loses the zest for life.

Tolstoy, the great Russian writer, said that he passed through it: "It all took place at a time when so far as my outward circumstances went, I ought to have been completely happy. I had a good wife who loved me and whom I loved; good children and large property which was increasing with no pains on my part. I was more respected by my kinsfolk and acquaintances than I had ever been; I was loaded with praise by strangers; and without exaggeration I could leave my life already famous. Moreover, I was not insane nor ill." He concludes by saying that life had lost all of its savor. He was lonely, until he found God.

On the level of ordinary life, there is perhaps more loneliness today than in any previous period of history. Children are lonely because they are teased, because of favoritism shown to others, because 5 million of them live in broken homes, or because their mothers are at work all day, returning at night to say as one mother did: "I had almost forgotten I had you."

Youths are lonely because they lack status; so they dress

like one another in order to be part of a crowd. Unmarried people are lonely because they are torn between self-giving and self-sufficiency; many married people are lonely together, like ships that pass in the night. One man came into a Bureau of Missing Persons and reported that his wife had been missing for fifteen years. He was asked why, in all that length of time, he had not reported her absence. His answer was: "I only now got lonesome."

The basic reason for loneliness is that man today has divorced himself from both love of God and love of neighbor. The peculiar characteristic about modern loneliness is that we can be in crowds and yet not be a part of them. There is no loneliness like the loneliness of a big city.

It is a paradox that in an age when men are determined to love only self, they hate to be alone. Men used to live for society. Now, living for the ego, they cannot stand their ego. One wants to be the master of one's ego, but one is so lonely with it.

The intelligentsia are often more lonely than the simple people because, having a greater pride and independence, they become authoritarian and inconsiderate in dealing with others; this increases their loneliness. They do nothing to love neighbor, but they still want to be loved. And nothing creates a vacuum like wanting to be loved. To demand love is to lose love. A selfish heart creates its own vacuum.

Would not a violin, if it were endowed with consciousness, be lonely if it did not know why it was made? One such unhinged soul who had completely lost a sense of vocation and destiny and purpose in life wrote his own epitaph later to be inscribed on his tombstone: "Born a human person. Died a wholesale grocer."

Every woman is beautiful when she is loved. There are some who have no beauty in themselves, but they become beautiful in the eyes of the beloved. This is the way we are in relationship to God. We take on an inner glow with the consciousness that we are loved. A husband can be responsible for his wife's premature aging, in the sense that she loses the beauty with which the husband once endowed her when he loved her. A sinner feels somewhat the same way without the love of God. His soul aches, wrinkles and cracks; he has broken the bond of love. The moment that he seeks to restore it, he becomes young again.

George Herbert in a poem entitled "The Pulley" reveals that the "dark wood" of loneliness is a path to God:

> *Yet with repining restlessness*
> *Let him be rich and weary;*
> *That at least,*
> *If goodness lead him not,*
> *Yet weariness may toss him to My breast.*

The Pious

It was Yeats who said that "today the good lack all conviction, while the worst are filled with passionate intensity." The evil are more zealous in spreading perversion than the good in soliciting conversion. The Gospel tells of a Pharisee who went to the Temple to tell God all the good things he did: how much he fasted and what large checks he made out to organized charities. Today, there are not many Pharisees who keep up a show of religion as so many did in the nineteenth century. Now the really good people rarely show their goodness. They keep their virtues for the temple and rarely show them before others. The Pharisee wanted everybody to know how good he was; good people today do not want anybody to know. It is the bad people today who want their badness to be known.

The result is a rift or a Great Divide between the light which ought to shine and does not, and the darkness which ought not to be prolonged but begins to preempt the day. Virtue is divorced from life, but evil lives in companionate marriage with it.

Applying this to our times, those who start with the equation that religion is a fraud or that the spiritual is a myth, never seem to have any encounter with evil.

We are not an irreligious country, nor is there a want of

a truly divine sentiment, or even a deep yearning of the sub-conscious for the Cross; but all of these things are divorced from life. We build gorgeous churches, but on Monday the parishioners go their separate ways; it would be very difficult to tell who in the bank, the factory or the office had acknowledged God on Sunday. There is practically no difference between the worshiper and the non-worshiper during the week. Do high school students who have religious training have any less enthusiasm for a synthetically Payola-made singer than one without catechism and prayers? May not the unbeliever be excused for saying: "If his faith means so little to him in business, in social life and in conversation, how could it make any difference in my life?"

Theologians write learned treatises about God and His relation to humanity, but they are so far removed from the dust of human lives and human misery as to make their intellectual deliverances nothing more than theory to the most of men.

As one writer has put it: "On the one side is the real life of mankind, dominated exclusively by material needs, instinctual reactions, intellect, by economic science and technology. And on the other side ignored, kept under wraps and ineffective, is the world of the spirit — a tiny corner or sanctuary of the heart where one piously preserves the immortal spiritual values." It could very well be that there is sometimes a deeper spiritual yearning in those who make no profession of religion, than there is in those who profess it on Sunday and ignore it from Monday to Saturday.

Those who have been blessed with the faith do not show it. As a result the spiritually starving seek an object of worship elsewhere. One may seek it in Communism not as an economic doctrine, but as an object of commitment, or in sex not because it satisfies, but because it is an intense feeling which makes him forget, for the moment, the purpose and value of life. Any religion, anything will do to fill up the void created by the loss of faith. This is met nowhere on a larger scale today than in Russia. One visitor said after his return from that country: "At the present time there is in Russia one problem, and it is the problem of the inner life, the moral life. As long as the heroic phase of the Revolution lasted, heroism took the place, as it were, of morality and it galvanized all emotions. But now that this has almost subsided, the eternal questions reappear.... In all the meetings, in all the student circles what are young men and young women discussing? Love, suffering and death." It could very well be that the religion-less are seeking religion more than the religious are showing theirs.

Do You Live Wholly for Yourself?

"No man is an island." This is one of the most quoted lines of the poet John Donne. To him every man is part of a vast continent. When, therefore, there is a death, one should not ask "for whom the bell tolls" — whence Hemingway derived the title of one of his novels. Donne says, "It tolls for thee."

In days of individualism when everyone proclaims "I must live my own life," there is apt to be a forgetfulness that there is no one whose life concerns himself alone. "None of us lives for oneself and no one dies for oneself."

It is this fact of our oneness with all human beings which invests life with such tremendous significance. If we could shut up within ourselves, so that what we did was nothing but that of an individual nomad whirling in space, we would then be truly individual, but this is not the case. Great forces have streamed into our lives from others, either to make us good or evil, also powerful influences flow out of our lives to contribute to the character formation of others.

The first question that was asked of man at the very beginning was: "Where is your brother?" It was Cain who tried to be an island to himself by asking: "Am I my brother's keeper?" We cannot turn away from a beggar without feeling that we have done wrong and failed in our duty. Every living man bears a relationship to all humanity.

His having lived will never cease to be felt throughout the universe. We own each other and God owns us all. A man never stands alone, unrelated to anything, because of his close relationship to the Creator Who made all. A willow tree may stand far from the stream, but its roots are burrowing down into the ground to gather its growth and its strength. As Plato said: "I was not born for myself alone, my country claims a part, my relations claim a part and my friends claim a part in me."

The sun, moon and stars are related and even the moon moves all the tides of the world. Scientists today agree that the universe is organic. As one of them told us, even the rattle that is dropped by a child from its cradle affects even the most distant star. If the physical universe is organic, then so much more are men organic one to another. Society is a vast network of reciprocal influences. That is why behind every delinquent child is a delinquent parent. That too is why eventually the law must take into account these sculptors who made such poor statues, namely, the father and mother. The rich who receive great advantages from society must also contribute to it. The United States, which is the richest country in the history of the world, owes an obligation to care for the poor in other parts of the world because they share our body and our blood.

The Eastern people tell us that we are part of all we meet, and all we do becomes part of us:

> There is a destiny which makes us brothers
> None makes his way alone:
> All we send into the lives of others
> Comes back into our own.

In a cemetery, a little white stone marks the grave of a little girl, and on the stone were chiseled these words: "A child of whom her playmates said: 'It was easier to be good when she was with us.'"

Be Unconscious

No woman is beautiful if she is conscious of being beautiful. A child who thinks he or she is "cute" is a brat. He who is conscious of his superiority is already a bore. A man who knows he is learned has more knowledge in his head than he has digested. He wears learning like a man might wear a two-pants suit: its excess shows. The difference between intellectuals and the intelligentsia is this: the intelligentsia are always out of touch with the common man; the intellectuals are not. The intelli-gentsia seek to impress; the intellectuals seek to help.

When one gets down to rock bottom, it would, therefore, seem that being unconscious of any good quality we possess is the condition of keeping that quality and making it effective with others. Learning that has not become part of oneself is like a woman walking the streets at noon in evening clothes. Poor boys who seek to convince others that they are rich must put on the trappings of luxury; the rich boy need not do so. The author who is conscious of being an author will cultivate the airs of author-ity, which our day requires: first, he must have a pipe in his mouth; secondly, he must be poorly dressed — generally with a shirt as multicolored as Joseph's coat and open at the neck; and finally he must have a copy of his book with the title showing, so that everyone can read it. His culture is showing like a ship in the night.

C.S. Lewis, one of the truly great writers and thinkers of our day, in an article entitled "Lilies that Fester," speaks of those who are consciously cultured. "When things of high value are easily destroyed, we must talk with great care, and perhaps the less we talk the better. To be constantly engaged with the ideal of 'culture' as something enviable or being meritorious, or something that confers prestige, seems to me to endanger those very 'enjoyments' for whose sake we chiefly value it. If we encourage others, or ourselves to hear, see or read great art on the ground that it is the *cultured* thing to do, we call into play precisely those elements in us which must be in abeyance before we can enjoy art at all. We are calling up the desire for self-improvement, the desire for distinction, the desire to revolt (from one group) and to agree (with another), and a dozen busy passions which, whether good or bad in themselves are, in relation to the arts simply a blinding and paralyzing distraction."

Of all the fields in which unconsciousness of possession of a talent or a gift is most important, it is in the field of religion. He who is consciously religious is not religious, but irreligious. The essence of being religious is to have one's attention and love centered on God and on neighbor. The difference between a religious man and a psychotic and neurotic resides precisely in this area, of how much the self is involved. While the man of faith is focused on God and neighbor, the mentally disturbed are radicated on their own ego. He who is very conscious of the fact that he is being very kind to his neighbor is not pious but an exhibitionist. The one in need to him is a foil, a "straight man" who gives him an opportunity to inflate his ego. Making any other human being a mirror in which we may have reflected back our own image is Narcissistic. Our neighbor is really a window, a transparent thing through which we see the thirsty and hungry Christ walking through the world. No image of self comes back; not only does the gift go out, but also the giver, and from that point on there is no consciousness of being good.

How rarely one finds in the lives of the saints any mention of their being religious or even of the word "religion." Our Blessed Lord never once used the word "religion." When St. James used it, it was a warning: "If anyone thinks he is religious... his religion is vain." The Pharisee in front of the temple was a consciously religious man; the publican in the back was not conscious at all that he was religious, but the Lord judged him so. The paradox goes even further. The man who is really spiritual has a sense of being very imperfect as Paul called himself "the worst of sinners." But this is because he is judging himself by the sun and not by the candle, by God's judgment and not by his neighbor's opinion, least of all his own. It could be that our constant analysis of the unconscious mind has made us very conscious of the thing of which we should be unconscious, namely, our goodness.

The Importance of Moral Character

The music we like is the music that we already have in our own soul. We hear a composition played for the first time, and we bring to it either our approval or disapproval. This is because our soul has its own melody, its tune, its rhythm, and it rejoices in that which conforms to it.

If one applies this to the moral order, it means that to the pure, all things are pure, and to the defiled all things are rotten.

A good man, like a bee, can extract honey from the bitterest plant, or like the aeolian harp, turn the shrieking wind into music. On the other hand, experience teaches that each man unerringly detects in others the vice with which he is most familiar in himself. Persons seem to each man what he is himself. One who suspects hypocrisy in the world is himself a hypocrite. He who is constantly afraid of being cheated is apt to be dishonest. The rotten apple is sweet to the worm, but nauseous to the palate of man. In trifling moods, all seems trivia. In serious moods, all seems solemn.

Each man, therefore, is to a great extent the creator of his own world, and the solution he brings to the world's problems will, to a great extent, depend upon his own inner condition. It will be found that those who lack a moral character will almost always find the fault in external environment. Communism recognizes no individual moral guilt except disloyalty to the Party. All ills are social. The individual is not to blame. By "the kettle calling the pot black," a defiled conscience thus escapes any necessity for moral betterment. Sometimes the excessive and violent interest in the transformation of externals is an escape from facing the necessity of moral reformation from within: Not everyone who becomes interested in social welfare does it for the best of motives. Sometimes, instead of reforming one's own conscience, one escapes into reforming everyone else's conscience.

There can also be another psychological outlet for a polluted conscience, namely, doing nothing. The guilty conscience on seeing the same wrongs done by others would have to condemn itself. To escape such a condemnation, the present tendency in courts and the social order is to blame muggings, murder, stealing, theft and violence on "sickness." This form of escapism has a less scientific foundation than a spiritual one, namely, how to get rid of one's own guilt. Both one's own moral corruption and the corruption of others are swallowed up in the denial of corruption. No one is guilty if he is "sick." It used to be that "charity covered a multitude of sins"; today sickness does it.

The Old Testament often speaks of prayers, almsgiving and sacrifice as being an abomination to the Lord. Why? Because they proceeded from a corrupt heart. A polluted person pollutes holy things.

The guilty conscience eventually becomes a violent conscience in the hope that, through it, goodness and virtue will be destroyed.

Virtue always humiliates the man who lacks it. In rare moments when goodness is gazed upon, we see our own wickedness.

Courtesy

A person who would generally be courteous to a stranger whom he met on the street will sometimes be discourteous at the wheel of an automobile. Perhaps the reason for the want of good manners in automobiles is an anonymity. Being unknown, our reputation suffers no disrepute in the eyes of others. It is also not uncommon to be kinder to the rich than to the poor, to a beautiful woman than to an ugly one, and to a blind man rather than to one who is deaf. Such actions are often less manifestations of courtesy than they are of the capricious actions of a carnal mind or an arbitrary rule imposed by the fashion of the times.

The word "courtesy" is derived from "court" and implied that refinement of manners which prevailed in the palaces of princes and distinguished the intercourse of the great. Later on, it came to mean any manner of affability with others. But true courtesy has an internal principle, namely, the seeing of the Divine in others. Perhaps one of the most courteous men who ever lived was Boaz. When he saw a poor woman, Ruth, gleaning in his fields, he told the workers to leave some "sheaves on purpose." The very triviality of his act is one of the earmarks of courtesy: "He who is faithful in little things will also be faithful in greater." Courtesy always has the power of descending into minute things and being attentive to little people, always doing more than the book of etiquette requires. It was said of Sir Walter Scott: "He speaks to every man as if they were blood relations."

One of the first rules of courtesy is: "Love without hypocrisy." Courtesy is not affectation but affection; not a mask that one wears to win the good repute of another but the service one renders to another because of the Divine Image in the soul. Courtesy of this kind is an imitation of the Love of God Who finds us lovable because He puts some of His Goodness into us. Continuing that benevolence, one puts love even in those who are unlovable, and thereby becomes courteous to them.

A second rule of courtesy: "Esteem others as better than yourselves." We know the worst of ourselves; we can only suspect the worst of others. We have always reason to respect others, for we can always believe them to be better than we are, seeing we cannot know them to be worse. Courtesy based on this lowliness of mind joins two virtues — that of humility and that of sympathy — from which results the identification with the feelings and interests of others, so as to make either their tears or their smiles our own. Courtesy, therefore, is the very opposite of the attitude: "I am as good as you."

One of the beautiful descriptions of a courteous gentleman was found in the writings of Newman: "he is one who never inflicts pain. He is mainly occupied in removing the obstacles which hinder the free and unembarrassed action of those about him and he concurs with their movements rather than takes the initiative himself. He carefully avoids whatever may cause a jar or a jolt in the minds of those with whom he is cast — all clashing of opinions or collision of feeling, all restraint or suspicion or gloom or resentment; his great concern being to make everyone at their ease and at home. He has his eyes on all his company; he is tender toward the bashful, gentle toward the distant, and merciful toward the absent. He guards against unseasonable allusions or topics which may irritate. He has no ears for slander or gossip, is scrupulous in imputing motives to those who interfere with him, and interprets everything for the best."

One of the greatest dangers to courtesy is familiarity. One half of the rudeness of children to parents and of husbands to wives and of wives to parents is due to the fact that familiarity has swallowed up gentleness. The best place for politeness is where we mostly think it superfluous. It is never a virtue if it is used only occasionally. The undisciplined are always discourteous; the saintly are always courteous. An American general during the Korean War described a missionary bishop who had survived several years in a Communist prison, and survived two death marches: "Whenever I saw him, he was carrying a man on his back." That is courtesy!

Courtesy
is not affectation but affection.

Judging Others

Human nature is something like a child's top painted in the variegated colors of the rainbow. When the top is at rest, each single color and tint can be distinguished, the red on one side, blue on another, white on the top, green on the bottom. When the top is set in motion and made to spin, darkness is suffused with brightness, brightness is mixed with darkness, the colors melt into a confused gray, until at last one knows not what color it be.

Judging our fellow men is something as perplexing as the judgment of colors on a spinning top. When a man is at rest, or in a fixed work, such as playing a game or working at a lathe, we think we can very well judge his character. But when we see him in the whirl and motion of everyday life, with its incessant change of pace, its rapid flash from one occupation or duty to another, all this goodness and badness blur into indistinctness. There is so much goodness at one moment, badness at another, sin in one instance, virtue in another, sobriety at one post, excess in another, that it is well to leave the judgment to God and to give the most charitable interpretation one can.

As Robert Burns wrote, begging that there be not severe judgment of one's fellow man:

Who made the heart, tis He alone
Decidedly can try us;
He knows each chord, its various tone,
Each spring, its various bias:
Then at the balance let's be mute,
We never can adjust it;
What's done we partly may compute,
But know not what's resisted.

Our Blessed Lord gave us one standard by which others may be judged; it was not a positive, but a negative one: "Judge not, and you shall not be judged. For as you have judged, so you will be judged, and the measure with which you measure will be measured out to you."

The way we judge others is very often the judgment which we pronounce upon ourselves. Whenever you find anyone who is hateful, censorious and bitter against those who lead religious lives, inquire not into his intellectual background; rather investigate his behavior. Those who condemned severely the woman in the Gospel and used her as a test case of the Mercy of Our Lord were themselves guilty of adultery. In all judgments, it is never so important to inquire *what* is said but *why* it is said. Every dramatist, scriptwriter, novelist and essayist who attacks the moral law has already lived against it in his own life. They may not know it, but in their writings they are penning their own autobiography. Those who satirize decency, who pour vitriolic acid on family life, who excuse militant atheism, are in the language of a poet "but a clod of warmer dust mixed with cunning sparks from hell."

Nero thought no person chaste because he was so unchaste himself. On the other hand, it will be found that those who are the most religious are those who are in the least censorious. A legend has it that one day an ambassador of God severely reprimanded a penitent. The former heard coming from the Crucifix the words: "I died for his sins, not you." It will invariably be found true that those who have suffered and who are saintly are always the most merciful to others. Not to be forgotten also are those who have received mercy and forgiveness themselves. One wonders if Saint Augustine was not one of the kindest and most compassionate of men, having been so tenderly touched by mercy after his sinful life.

Adelaide Ann Proctor, pleading for sympathetic understanding of souls that have fallen, writes:

> *The fall thou darest to despise —*
> *May be the angel's slackened hand*
> *Has suffered it, that he may rise*
> *And take a firmer, surer stand;*
> *Or, trusting less to earthly things,*
> *May henceforth learn to use his wings.*

> *"Judge not,*
> *and you shall not be judged."*

Forgiveness

Forgiveness has always existed in the world. But one wonders if forgiveness does not decline with a consciousness of moral guilt. If I am incapable of doing wrong, then I can never expect forgiveness. That is why the denial of guilt is the unforgivable sin. If I am blind and deny either my blindness or the vision of others, how shall I ever want to see? It will also be noted how much more readily those who have their sins forgiven are willing to extend the courtesy to others, while those who excuse their thefts and adulteries as an inherited Oedipus complex are always hard on the offending neighbor. The penitent forgives other penitents for their sakes and the impenitent for his sake.

Forgiveness appears in some by not returning hate with hate; in others, by the inner waiving of a legitimate right to revenge. But it reaches its peak when no external circumstance is permitted to excuse pardoning others.

In the parable of the Good Samaritan there was this universalization of the family relationship. Race, profession, nationality were not permitted to obscure the need of helping an "enemy." Peter set a limit to pardon. He was willing to forgive seven times, but the Lord told him to be prepared to forgive seventy times seven, which is not 490 but infinitely.

One of the most beautiful things about forgiveness is that it can evoke love where there was none before. It then becomes imitative of God's way with us Who loves us "while we were yet sinners." We pardon as we love. Since God loves infinitely, He pardons without limit.

Forgiveness has a strong redemptive power. George Bernard Shaw stated a truth of this kind when he put those words upon the lips of Joan of Arc when she was sent to the faggots: "If I go through the fire, I shall go to the hearts of the people." Somehow or other, by not bearing revenge against those who persecuted her, she eventually won all the hearts of France. Men's persuasions and explanations and devices may fail, but the love that was shown by forgiveness first manifested on the Cross is the simplest way to the human heart.

In the light of the eternal judgment, he who refuses to forgive others breaks down the bridge over which he himself must pass, for everyone has need to be forgiven. The Divine Law is that only those who forgive will be forgiven. It is much easier to forgive the weak who have injured us or those who are beneath us in dignity than it is to forgive the powerful or the better or the nobler whom we have injured. It will generally be found that when the person who has been injured is nobler than oneself, a deep resentment often follows. He who has gone so far to cut out the claws of the lion will not feel himself secure until he has drawn out his teeth. In this truth is hidden the explanation of why the Divine Who came to bring forgiveness to humans was crucified at the moment of greatest forgiveness. Though the Divine forgiveness comes to those who forgive, nevertheless, some say: "I cannot forgive myself." As Cardinal Newman answered: "No true penitent forgets or forgives himself; an unforgiving spirit towards himself is the very price of God's forgiving him." Of course, no man can forgive himself. He can only be forgiven by Him Whom he has injured. When we injure a fellow man, sometimes it takes a lifetime to be restored to his good graces. But the Lord forgives with a tear. Joy and sorrow have the same fountain — tears. The most beautiful mystery of religion is this: "If we had never sinned, we could never call Jesus, 'Savior'."

> *In the light of eternal judgment,*
> *he who refuses to forgive others*
> *breaks down the bridge over which*
> *he himself must pass.*

Sympathy

"Write a check!" This is one of the most common expressions of men who are called generous and philanthropic, when asked to subscribe for a cause or to build a field house or a laboratory. They discharge the appeal by a stroke of a pen. While the immediacy of giving is very much to be commended, and while it never fails to rejoice the recipient, there is often wanting a spiritual quality which affects both the check writer and the check endorser. This is particularly true of very large donations. Andrew Carnegie, who gave away millions, once said that he never missed anything that he gave away, first because he did not know how much he had; second, all that he gave away was paper and he could never notice any decrease in his paper, by which he meant checks, stocks, bonds, etc.

The nature of giving is best illustrated in the life of Our Blessed Lord Who one day was approached by a leper who asked for healing. The Gospel tells us that Our Lord "stretched out His Hand and touched" the leper. The Savior could have healed without the touch, as He healed the servant of the Centurion at a distance. Why, then, in the face of one of life's greatest miseries, and a disease from which the healthy often recoil, did the Lord cure with a touch?

Because of a spiritual quality in the Giver; namely,

compassion or the ability to suffer with others. Touch is the language of love. There are actually three intimacies in love: hearing, seeing and touching. We could never love anyone unless we first know him or hear his voice. Next, after hearing a voice, one wishes to see the person. Vision is the second intimacy. Then finally, there comes the greatest of all intimacies, which only a few may enjoy, and that is the intimacy of touch. The Son of God made Man touched the leper in order to annihilate distance between the Giver and the receiver, between the Lover and the beloved, to prove sympathy by contact, to identify Himself with the woes of others. How different was the attitude of Shylock who said: "I will buy with you, sell with you, talk with you, walk with you... but I will not eat with you, drink with you, nor pray with you."

According to the Old Testament Law, Our Blessed Lord would have become ceremonially unclean until that evening because He touched the leper. How could He justify His exemption from the Law? Because the priests of the Old Testament in their contact with the leper were judged exempt from the law of defilement. How much more was He the great High Priest and the Law Giver in cleansing the leper. Our Lord, however, did conform Himself to the Law, inasmuch as He ordered the leper to show himself to the priest in order that his cleanness might be authoritatively certified, thus restoring him again to society.

The Hand that touched was also the Hand that later on would be pierced with a nail, because He would take upon Himself the human leprosy of sin. The point is, however, that the hand was the extension of His personality and, therefore, a sign of His intimate compassion with the leper. Man is the only creature that has a hand that is creative, and with it he puts the stamp of his mind upon stone and gold, founds his sovereignty of civilization and comforts his fellow man.

There was another moral effect equally important about touching; namely, the affection bestowed on the leper. Every diseased person has a heart, and the physician who heals the body as if it were a guinea pig but awakens no human love in the heart has failed in his mission as a healer. That leper was ostracized from society. He had need of a sip of the milk of human kindness. Up to that point the leper was despised and rejected. Now he was loved by Love.

Sometimes "writing a check" can be just as cold as flinging a dime at a beggar. The gift of the lover without the love of the giver is bare. It is part of my work to gather alms to support over 400 leper colonies throughout the world. In twelve years in this work, we have never received a large check. Every gift was a sacrifice, something hard to give, something that demanded self-denial. In every single gift there was, therefore, a compassion with the suffering of the lepers, and also a communication of love. Sometimes those who have little to give, give with greater love, for after the example of the Master, they too "touch the leper."

> Sometimes "writing a check"
> can be just as cold
> as flinging a dime at a beggar.
> The gift of the lover
> without the love of the giver
> is bare.

The Way
of Blessedness

There is hope for each of us.…
Every man is made to the image and likeness of God.

The Beatitudes

This is the first of several chapters on the Beatitudes. One hears it endlessly repeated that the essence of all religion is to be found in the Beatitudes. To some extent this is true, but those who say this little realize that the Beatitudes represent the most revolutionary doctrine ever preached. The history of the world can be told in the story of two mountains: one is the mountain on which the Beatitudes were preached; the other mountain previewed what happens to him who practices the Beatitudes, namely, the Mount of Calvary. The conclusion is inescapable: he who activates the Beatitudes in his own life will draw upon himself the wrath of the world.

The day Our Lord taught the Beatitudes He signed His own death warrant. The sound of nails and hammers digging through human flesh were the echoes thrown back from the mountainside where He told men how to be happy or blessed. Everybody wants to be happy; but His ways were the very opposite of the ways of the world.

One way to make enemies and antagonize people is to challenge the spirit of the world. The world has a spirit, as each age has a spirit. There are certain unanalyzed assumptions which govern the conduct of the world. Anyone who challenges these worldly maxims, such as "You only live once," "Get as much out of life as you can," "Who will ever know about it?" "What is sex for, if not for pleasure?" is bound to make himself unpopular.

In the Beatitudes, Our Divine Lord takes those flimsy catchwords of the world: "security," "revenge," "laughter," "popularity," "getting even," "sex," "armed might" and "comfort" — and turns them upside down. To those who say: "Laugh and the world laughs with you," He says: "Blessed are those who mourn." To those who say: "If nature gave you sex instincts, you ought to give them free expression, otherwise you will become frustrated," He says: "Blessed are the clean of heart." To those who say: "Seek to be popular and well known," He says: "Blessed are you when men revile you and persecute you and speak all manner of evil against you falsely because of Me." To those who say: "In time of peace, prepare for war," He says: "Blessed are the peacemakers."

The cheap cliches around which movies are written and novels composed, He scorns. He proposes to burn what they worship; to conquer errant sex instincts instead of allowing them to make slaves of man; to tame economic conquests instead of making happiness consist of an abundance of things external to the soul. All false beatitudes which make happiness depend on self-expression, license, having a good time or "Eat, drink and be merry for tomorrow you die," He scorns because they bring mental disorders, unhappiness, false hopes, fears and anxieties.

Those who would escape the impact of the Beatitudes say that Our Divine Savior was a creature of His time, but not of ours, and that, therefore, His words do not apply to us. He was not a creature of His time, nor of any time; but we are! Mohammed belonged to his time; hence he said that a man could have concubines in addition to four wives at one time. Mohammed belongs even to our time, because moderns say that a man can have many wives, if he drives them in tandem style, one after another. But Our Lord did not belong to His day, any more than He belonged to ours. To marry one age is to be a widow in the next. Because He suited no age, He was the model for all ages. He never used a phrase that depended on the social order in which He lived; His Gospel was no easier then than it is now.

The Beatitudes and Happiness

Everyone wants to be happy. All men are agreed on this. The difficulty is to decide what happiness is. What may be happiness for the body is not necessarily happiness for the mind. What may give immediate pleasure does not necessarily give peace of soul, and what is true for time may be false for eternity. The Beatitudes represent the Divine way to be happy, though they are completely at variance with the attitudes of the world.

The Greek word for happiness used in the Beatitudes is "*makarios.*" It was a word originally applied to Divinity; for example, the Greeks always called their gods "the Blessed Ones." The New Testament twice uses the word as applied to God Himself. Hence, the word "blessed" in the Beatitudes is less a statement than an exclamation, and refers to a promised bliss, which is nothing else than the perfect bliss of God Himself.

Carlyle in *Sartor Resartus* distinguishes between the happiness of the Beatitudes and carnal happiness: "I asked myself: What is this that, ever since earliest years, thou has been fretting, and fuming and lamenting and self-tormenting on account of? Say it in a word: is it not because thou art not HAPPY? Because Thou (sweet gentleman) art not sufficiently honored, nourished, soft-bedded and lovingly cared for? Foolish soul! What act of Legislature was there that thou shoudst be Happy? There is in man a desire for something HIGHER than love of happiness: Was it not to preach forth this same HIGHER that sages and martyrs, the poet and the priest, in all times, have spoken and suffered; hearing testimony, through life and through death, of the Godlike that is in man and how in the Godlike only has he Strength and Freedom."

The key to the Sermon on the Mount is the way Our Lord used two expressions: one was, "You have heard." The other was the short, emphatic word, "But." When He said, "You have heard," He reached back to what human ears had heard for centuries and still hear from ethical reformers — all those rules and codes and precepts which are half measures between instinct and reason, between local customs and the highest ideals.

"You have heard that it was said, 'You shall not commit adultery.'" Moses had said it; pagan tribes suggested it; primitive peoples respected it. Then came the terrible and awful "but": "But I tell you. . . ." "But I tell you that he who casts his eye on a woman so as to lust after her, has already committed adultery with her in his own heart." Our Lord went into the soul and laid hold of thought, and branded even the *desire* for sin as a sin. If it was wrong to do a certain thing, it was wrong to think about that thing. He would say, "Away with your hygiene which tries to keep hands clean after they have stolen, and bodies free from disease after they have ravished another." He went into the depths of the heart and branded even the intention to sin a sin. He did not wait for the evil tree to bear evil fruit. He would prevent the very sowing of the evil seed. Wait not until your hidden sins come out as psychoses and neuroses and compulsions. Get rid of them at their sources. Repent! Purge! Evil that can be put into statistics or that can be locked in jails is too late to remedy.

The Commandments were given to Moses alone, with God hidden in the darkness and with the people off at a distance. The Beatitudes were given by Our Lord, sitting in the midst of His Apostles and surrounded by the multitudes. The Law was given to a particular nation and spirit; the Beatitudes to all mankind. The Law was given amidst thunder and lightning; the Beatitudes in calmness and peace on a grassy hillside.

The Beatitudes represent
the Divine way to be happy.

Blessed Are the Poor in Spirit

The first beatitude of the world is: "Blessed are the rich, for they shall be able to buy many things and have many pleasures." The first Beatitude of the Sermon on the Mount is: "Blessed are the poor in spirit, for theirs is the Kingdom of Heaven."

First, consider Him Who spoke these words. Let the Lord become man and come into a world which believes in the primacy of the economic, the supremacy of the dollar, the happiness of clipping stocks and bonds, the thrill of counting profits and adding barn to barn — and see what will happen to Him. He will be so poor that during life He will have nowhere to lay His Head, and in His last hour, He will be so impoverished that they will strip Him of His garments and give Him a stranger's grave for His burial, as they gave Him a stranger's stable for His birth.

In the original language of the Gospel, what did Our Lord mean by the poor? There were two Greek words for "poor." One was *"ptochos"* meaning one who is so poor that he earns his livelihood generally by begging. This is the word that was used to describe the beggar Lazarus, covered with sores, who sat at the gate of the rich man. The other Greek word to describe the poor was *"penes"* and refers to one who is so poor that he earns his bread by daily labor, and is without superfluities. The Greek word used is the former, and therefore implies a beggar who is destitute. But it is not to be forgotten that it is the "poor in spirit" who are declared blessed, or the happy ones of the earth. Our Lord here affirms the happiness of those who are in their own spirit absolutely devoid of wealth. It is an attitude of the soul not toward economic conditions.

From this it follows that poverty of spirit is a profound realization in a person of his utter helplessness and beggary, as far as any true worth is concerned. Spiritual beggars bring nothing to God but their complete emptiness and the need to stoop in the dust for grace and mercy. This is a conception of life that is absolutely original, never having entered into the thoughts of ancient poets or sages; namely, the placing of poverty in the spirit and making it identical with human destitution in the face of the richness of God.

As a man is poor economically who is destitute of all things needful for the body, so he is poor spiritually when he has a sense of utter want and helplessness in relation to his soul. Spiritual poverty corresponds to that psychological state of the prodigal son at the moment when he turned back again to his father's house; namely, he began to be "in want."

Only those who are conscious of their own inner nudity are willing to take the place of beggars to receive true riches from the hand of Divine Charity. Thus, "the poor have the Gospel preached to them" means that they hear it not with their own ears but with their souls, for their want of egotism and pride opens them to the meaning of spiritual riches.

When a man loses his egotism and boastfulness and con- ceit, when he sees his hands empty of all deeds that are really good, then and only then does he know that he can take into his hands a love that he can never merit, that he need not lose, and that he belongs to a kingdom where nothing can break his peace or steal his joy.

Blessed Are the Meek

The world too has its beatitudes, the second of which is: "Blessed are the hard-boiled, for they never let life hurt them," or "Blessed are they who stand up for their rights and never take things lying down." As soon as one hears the contrary Beatitude of the Sermon on the Mount: "Blessed are the meek, for they shall inherit the earth," one is at first inclined to interpret it as weakness, spineless submissiveness and a readiness to be walked on.

This is what happened to Him Who preached it. Let Him come into a world which proclaims the Gospel of the strong, and advocate gentleness even toward enemies, and He will one day feel the scourges of strong barbarians laid across His back; He will be struck on the cheek by a mocking fist during one of His trials; He will see men take a sickle and cut the grass from a hill on Calvary, and then use a hammer to pinion Him to a Cross, to test the meekness, and see if He Who endures the worst that evil has to offer, could eventually love executioners by pardoning them.

What does meekness mean? It does not mean passivity in the face of opposition, and above all, it does not mean weakness. The Greek word which is used in the Gospel, *"praotes,"* is not a gentleness which has its source in weakness, but rather a gentleness which has its source in strength. It is that of a giant who wrestles with a child without hurting him, or of a powerful monarch who uses only enough strength to put down opposition, or a God Incarnate Who could have smitten His enemies in the Temple who were buying and selling, but contented Himself to opening a few cages and driving the traders out with ropes.

Meekness is disciplined strength, not cowardly weakness. Moses is described as the meekest man on earth, and yet at one time he was one of the most fiery tempered individuals, having killed an Egyptian and broken, in his anger, the two stone tablets on which the Law had been written. The meek man does not retaliate injuries, but rather forgives them, as Christ on the Cross said: "Father, forgive them for they know not what they do." He takes insult calmly when He is falsely accused as Our Lord remained silent before Pilate. Natural meekness may be no better than timidity or shyness or weakness of character. But the meekness of the Beatitude is that which is God-inspired, and which is a quiet strength which wins its way when violence fails, exerting a strong influence over rougher characters.

Meekness which belongs to the natural or psychological order is allied with timidity or insensibility, but this meekness which is born of the Spirit is a Divine product and requires great self-control. As Browning said: "The meek man is the one who knows well what it is to have a giant's strength, but he also knows that it is tyrannous to use it as a giant." The meek man is one who, under Divine inspiration, goes through life taking the poison from every sting, receiving upon his shield of faith every dart, and even looking lovingly on those who betray, such as the Savior looked on Peter.

This is the kind that inherit the earth, with a gladness and a happiness which the selfish and dissatisfied and proud men can never know. St. Augustine said: "Do you wish to possess the earth? Beware then lest you be possessed by it." The meek man will have no civil claim to the earth; that is, before men and its courts. But he will have a spiritual claim to it which only the spiritual can understand for they "having nothing, possess all things." Being devoid of all inordinate care for the world, they, in a certain sense, possess it. Our powers of dispossession are greater than our powers of possession. We cannot take the whole earth in our hand, but we can wash our hands of the earth. In wanting nothing, by a peculiar paradox, one has all things — provided the soul is meek and humble of heart.

Blessed Are the Clean of Heart

Another beatitude of the world is: "Blessed is sex, for through it you will have free expression and avoid frustration."

The Beatitude of the God-man is: "Blessed are the clean of heart, for they shall see God." It goes back to one of the most beautiful stories of the Old Testament when Moses asked to see the glory of God. God told him that it was impossible, for no one could look upon Him face to face. God, however, conceded to Moses a view of Him as it were, passing through the cleft of a rock. But all that Moses saw was merely the retreating procession of God, not the vision of one advancing face to face.

In the Old Testament purity was principally a matter of observing certain rituals and ceremonies, but in this Beatitude purity is centered in the heart and the attitude of the soul. The very fact that the vision of God is promised to the pure in heart means that there are some to whom this boon cannot be given. The vision is spiritual and depends not on what is outside of the eye, but on what is inside of the heart.

This is true even psychologically. Moral character and the state of a man's mind makes a difference to what he sees. It is too often assumed that a right understanding of God depends upon education and intellectual training. This Beatitude insists that there is a moral as well as an intellectual condition of coming to the knowledge of God. Most people are kept from Him not just because of difficulties they have with the Creed, but rather because of difficulties they have with the Commandments. It is not in the way they *think*, but in the way they *act* that they become crossed up.

A keen spiritual observer will inquire just as rapidly into a man's behavior as into his concepts. Each day of life we are either fitting ourselves for the vision of God or else blinding ourselves to it. The sun may be outside of the window, but if we keep the blinds down the light cannot come in. As Our Blessed Lord said: "You will not come to Me because your lives are evil." Actually, the frustrated, miserable unhappy souls in the world are those who have clouded their character by a failure to see that sex is a mystery, that it is a continuation of the creativity of God and only when used within His holy purposes does it give full satisfaction both to body and soul.

Friends are not seen only by the eyes of the body. The friend that one loves is discerned spiritually, known by his truth and the nobility of his character, which the senses cannot see. Purity, likewise, gives communion with the loving Spirit of the Father, and brings to us an understanding and love of Him.

The vision of the soul has something to do with the afflictions of the heart. Try to tell an egotist the beauty of unselfishness. You might as well tell a deaf man about the harmony of a Beethoven. Telling the carnal man about purity and its rewards is telling the blind of color. The man whose heart is unholy sees not God. To the impure, nothing is pure, for he carries defilement with him. To be pure in heart is to see purity everywhere. The pure of heart shall see God in nature's mirror and in science, in creation's visions and in the voices of every color. They will see Him in His Providence. They will even see Him in the mysteries they cannot understand.

Blessed Are the Merciful

A beatitude of the world is: "Blessed is the man who looks after himself first." Sartre has given the final expression to this by enunciating the beatitude: "My neighbor is hell."

The opposite key to happiness pronounced by the Lord of the Universe was: "Blessed are the merciful, for they shall obtain mercy."

This Beatitude represents a tremendous development over the Commandments. Of the Ten Commandments, three were concerned with justice to God and seven with justice to neighbor. There is not great mercy demanded. The Old Testament, when it speaks of mercy, usually applies it to God, though there be individual instances of mercy in men, such as the mercy Abraham showed to his nephew Lot, as Joseph manifested to his brethren, and Moses to his sister Miriam after she had rebelled against him and the Lord had smitten her with leprosy, and the mercy extended to David after his sin. In the Old Testament the Hebrew word for mercy, "*hesed*," occurs about 150 times and in nine-tenths of these occasions refers to the Mercy of God.

But in the Beatitude: "Blessed are the merciful for they shall receive mercy," the recommendation is for men to imitate the mercy of God. The same attitude of mercy which God has to man, now man is to show to his fellow man. The reason is not because he is deserving of the mercy he receives from God, but because he is not deserving. No human being ever merited that God should become man and pay the debt of his sin; having thus received so much undeserved forgiveness, man must be ready to extend it to others.

One wonders if one of the effects of the modern denial of guilt is not to effect a decline of mercy and forgiveness to others. One finds this idea expressed in one of the writings of Nathaniel Hawthorne. A very human Miriam says to her friend Hilda: "You have no sin nor any conception of what it is; therefore, you are so terribly severe. As an angel you are not amiss, but as a human creature, you need a sense of sin to soften you."

May not a bluntness, a want of courtesy and politeness, quick answers, darting retorts, inconsiderateness of the feelings of others, be due in part to the fact that modern man, having denied that he is ever guilty of sin, thinks himself as never in need of mercy? Having never been touched by its healing hand, why should he ever extend it to others?

The mercy of this Beatitude is not a natural, psychological or emotional generosity to others, particularly to those we love. "For you love those who love you; do not the heathens do the same?" Nor is it a humanitarian affection, for it is very easy to love humanity, but to love this particular man who is always sniffling or interrupting a conversation or blowing smoke in your eyes, this requires much more than a natural sense of human worth. To be kind to the beautiful and not to the ugly, to the rich and not the poor, cannot be a love of neighbor, but a love of self.

To be merciful is to have the same attitude toward men

as God has, to think of men as God thinks of them, to feel for men as God feels for them, and to act toward them as God acts toward them. Though the inspiration for mercy comes from that of Christ, there is the added truth that if we would be forgiven, we must forgive. This is insisted on in the Lord's Prayer; it is the moral of the parable of the debtors in which he who was forgiven a great debt choked a neighbor who owed him a few pence. Hence, the Scripture says: "Judgment is without mercy to him who has not shown mercy."

Mercy, like all other virtues, is its own reward, for a well of sweetness is opened up in our own hearts and even in the world round about us:

> *The song is to the singer, and comes back most to him;*
> *The gift is to the giver, and comes back most to him;*
> *The love is to the lover, and comes back most to him;*
> *It cannot fail.*

The Blessedness of the Starving Soul

The beatitude of the world spoken on the Plain of the Commonplace is: "Blessed are the blasé, for they never worry over their sins." In contrast with this is the Beatitude pronounced on the Mountain: "Blessed are they who hunger and thirst for holiness; they shall have their fill." Let the Lord of the Universe come into this world which denies absolute truth, which says that right and wrong are only questions of a point of view, that one must be broad-minded about virtue and vice, and let Him say to the world: "Blessed are they who hunger and thirst after holiness which I am —." He will find that in their broad-mindedness they will give the mob the choice of Him or Barabbas; they will crucify Him with thieves and try to make the world believe that God is no different from a batch of robbers who are His bedfellows in death.

This Beatitude follows those in which there is a recognition of our own poverty and nothingness and, as a result, a longing for betterment surges in the soul. As the heart pants after the living waters, so do the spiritually thirsty yearn to drink of the waters of life. This Beatitude is not for the dilettantes or the blasé or the self-righteous, who are their own creators, their own redeemers, or who live on the surface of their souls with no great passion; it is not for the spiritually poor who do not wish to be rich, nor for the morally sick who will not be healed; rather it is the Beatitude which issues challenges such as the Lord issued to the rich young man, asking him if he was willing to give up his luxuries for the "passionless passion" which the world can never give.

This Beatitude offers a great deal of hope, for it is addressed not to those who have *attained* holiness, but for those who have not, or who "hunger and thirst for holiness." There is a blessedness in the longing, in the striving for betterment, in the getting up after the fall, in making oneself a sheep which gets out of the mud rather than a pig which stays in it; it addresses itself to all pagans who stumble in darkness and yet aspire to the light, to those who have a fragment or a segment of the circle of truth and would complete its full orb, for those who are in the clutches of sin and through satiety no longer want a food which makes hungry where most are satisfied. It beckons to those who are sick of mediocrity and ordinariness, and who see in the little spark of human love which they enjoy something that has been thrown off from the great flame of love, Which is God. It is for those who want to be good and who realize the nobility that is in the depths of their souls and, above all, for those who are full of husks and are very empty.

But there is a catch to this longing for holiness. It may not be a mere emotionalism on the surface of the soul, nor a vague humanitarian cry for more culture. It is a longing which must be as poignant and as terrible and as driving as hunger and thirst. The craving can only be compared to that of the passion of a starving man for food and of parched lips for water. Some can be ill and feel as if they were hungry, and yet when food is offered they are unable to eat. So there are some that can have an emptiness, but when true holiness is presented to them, they turn their souls away. Such refusal to satisfy the hunger of their souls often ends in an atrophy to the deadness to the Bread of Life.

The desire, therefore, is not just for earthly happiness, but for holiness which is in Love Who walked the earth. But this Beatitude promises that the desire shall not be mocked, nor find itself empty and hollow. There shall be a filling without being sated. Body hunger and thirst are appetites that return frequently and require fresh satisfaction. But these holy desires rest not in anything that is attained, but push on further to renewed pardons, fresher supplies of life and truth and love, ever fulfilling the words of Augustine:

Our hearts were made for Thee, O Lord,
and they are restless until they rest in Thee.

ST PAULS

This book was produced by ST PAULS, the publishing house operated by the Society of St. Paul, an international religious congregation of priests and brothers dedicated to serving the Church through the communications media.

For information regarding this and associated ministries of the Pauline Family of Congregations, write to the Vocation Director, Society of St. Paul, 2187 Victory Blvd., Staten Island, New York 10314-6603. Phone us at 718-865-8844.

E-mail:vocation@stpauls.us
www.vocationoffice.org

That the Word of God be everywhere known and loved.